TIMOTHY DONNELLY

WAVE BOOKS SEATTLE AND NEW YORK

THE

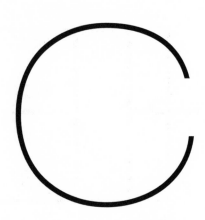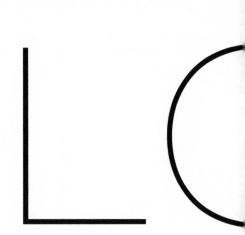

RAT

Published by Wave Books

www.wavepoetry.com

Wave Books titles are distributed to the trade by

Consortium Book Sales and Distribution

Phone: 800-283-3572 / SAN 631-760X

This title is available in limited edition hardcover

directly from the publisher

Library of Congress Cataloging-in-Publication Data

Donnelly, Timothy.

The cloud corporation / Timothy Donnelly. — 1st ed.

p. cm.

ISBN 978-1-933517-47-6 (pbk. : alk. paper)

I. Title.

PS3604.O5637C56 2010

811'.6—dc22

2010013946

Designed and composed by Quemadura

Printed in the United States of America

9 8 7 6 5 4

Wave Books 024

CONTENTS

1

2

3

4

FOR LYNN MELNICK

Sometimes a thousand twangling instruments

Will hum about mine ears; and sometime voices,

That if I then had wak'd after long sleep,

Will make me sleep again, and then in dreaming,

The clouds methought would open, and show riches

Ready to drop upon me, that when I wak'd,

I cried to dream again.

THE NEW
INTELLIGENCE

After knowledge extinguished the last of the beautiful
fires our worship had failed to prolong, we walked
back home through pedestrian daylight, to a residence

humbler than the one left behind. A door without mystery,
a room without theme. For the hour that we spend
complacent at the window overlooking the garden,

we observe an arrangement in rust and gray-green,
a vagueness at the center whose slow, persistent
movements some sentence might explain if we had time

or strength for sentences. To admit that what falls
falls solitarily, lost in the permanent dusk of the particular.
That the mind that fear and disenchantment fatten

comes to boss the world around it, morbid as the damp-
fingered guest who rearranges the cheeses the minute the host
turns to fix her a cocktail. A disease of the will, the way

false birch branches arch and interlace from which
hands dangle last leaf-parchments and a very large array
of primitive bird-shapes. Their pasted feathers shake

in the aftermath of the nothing we will ever be content
to leave the way we found it. I love that about you.
I love that when I call you on the long drab days practicality

keeps one of us away from the other that I am calling
a person so beautiful to me that she has seen my awkwardness
on the actual sidewalk but she still answers anyway.

I say that when I fell you fell beside me and the concrete
refused to apologize. That a sparrow sat for a spell
on the windowsill today to communicate the new intelligence.

That the goal of objectivity depends upon one's faith
in the accuracy of one's perceptions, which is to say
a confidence in the purity of the perceiving instrument.

I won't be dying after all, not now, but will go on living dizzily
hereafter in reality, half-deaf to reality, in the room
perfumed by the fire that our inextinguishable will begins.

THE MALADY
THAT TOOK
THE PLACE
OF THINKING

When I close my eyes its voice insists we're close
to solving once and for all and with panache
those mysteries to which we've been applying

ourselves so much these days, almost to the exclusion
of all that I had taken to be the case, factwise.
There had seemed to be only one world to adhere to

but now I can see how there really isn't any, just roads
with signs directing further, towards and away
from the same humiliating noplace you already are.

These mysteries will be solved not one at a time
but in a slow, general unfolding along the lines
of the magnolia, and trying to rush one solution by prying it

open will compromise not only this solution but many
if not all the others. I'm not that person anymore
with his hands immediately all over the magnolia.

I'm not that other one either, stomping off sorry
he doesn't understand. If it looks like I'm thinking, I'm not,
I'm waiting, and I can wait forever to find out why.

If it looked like I was sorry to look at that photograph
of women and children shot down by an American
battalion on a bright clear day in March, look again:

with no world to adhere to, there can be no photograph,
no women, no children, and certainly no battalion
shooting when there was nothing there to begin with.

mysterious   ＊ Allen Watts - writer

This is one of Donnellys poems that I really enjoyed.
What is "thinking"?
  - Thinking is the act of generating thoughts and it is what
  happens everyday.
What is the value of thinking?
  - Thinking is crucial to everyday life because without it,
  we wouldnt have any guide, compass, or opinion
  in life. Personally, I am the biggest overthinker. I think
  way too much

Malady ——— Thinking/consciousness
  | - subconscious
disease   · internal
                    warning system

- generative   " who beats your heart?"
- inherent   " who's in control of your mind?"
- consideration   what is your consciousness?
- out of your control or   · your consciousness is your
  in your control?   inner core and your involuntary
                              being → mindfulness/meditation

TO HIS DEBT

Where would I be without you, massive shadow
dressed in numbers, when without you there

behind me, I wouldn't be myself. What wealth
could ever offer loyalty like yours, my measurement,

my history, my backdrop against which every
coffee and kerplunk, when all the giddy whoring

around abroad and after the more money money
wants is among the first things you prevent.

My phantom, my crevasse—my emphatically
unfunny hippopotamus, you take my last red cent

and drag it down into the muck of you, my
sassafras, my Timbuktu, you who put the kibosh

on fine dining and home theater, dentistry and work
my head into a lather, throw my ever-beaten

back against a mattress of intractable topography
and chew. Make death with me: my sugar

boat set loose on caustic indigo, my circumstance
dissolving, even then—how could solvency

hope to come between us, when even when I dream
I awaken in an unmarked pocket of the earth

without you there—there you are, supernaturally
redoubling over my shoulder like the living

wage I never make, but whose image I will always
cling to in the negative, hanged up by the feet

among the mineral about me famished like a bat
whose custom it is to make much of my neck.

THE NEW HYMNS

* newness
- old hymn vs new

They all begin by commanding you to praise
things like sea-thistle, pinecones, a crate of tangerines
stacked into a ziggurat like one you envision

ticking under overgrowth, ancient and counting
down deep in the tropics until at last a certain
heavenly alignment triggers doomsday, what then?

To think nothing might feel good for a time, the way
walking can, just moving around, turning
right whenever you happen to, heading along

toward nowhere in particular, getting there almost
without really trying or memory of where
you started out from, much less how you'll ever get back.

I don't want to have to. I don't want to have to
locate divinity in a loaf of bread, in a sparkler,
or in the rainlike sound the wind makes through

mulberry trees, not tonight. Listen to them carry on
about gentleness when it's inconceivable
that any kind or amount of it will ever be able to

balance the scales. I have been held down
by the throat and terrified, numb enough to know.
The temperature at which no bird can thrive—

a lifelong feeling that I feel now, remembering
down the highway half-hypnotized in the
backseat feeling what I feel now, and moderate

happiness has nothing to do with it: I want to press
my face against the cold black window until
there is a deity whose only purpose is to stop this.

what stood out to you?
 - It was a very depressing and somber tone
" I don't want to have to."
  ↳ how does this feeling of obligations and requirements
    make you feel?
  - I honestly feel this sometimes too especially in my
    college schedule. It seems restricting and even though
    we dont want to do something, we still have to.
    ↳ wanting freedom, freedom of choice
  - Freedom free will -hypocricy, coercion
  - the idea of images that aren't holy that we think are
    holy.

" New hymn"
  ↳ different from the stereotypical "old" hymn. Although
    its not religious, she is a icon right now and an
    inspiration to many.
another hymn (people/athletes)
  Micheal Jordan - Micheal Phelps, Taylor swift
  Messi   } find 2
                                                       videos for
objects in our culture: both as
  • skincare products   sources
  • supplements/viatimins
      ↳ constantly being presented with
        stuff and people who are our "Gods"
      [telling us what value is
      ↳ what are we giving our energy to?

BETWEEN
THE RIVERS

Maybe there's a stage in wakefulness like standing up
on a rooftop I've never quite been able to figure out
how to get to, and it's from this stage that everyone
keeps shouting at me saying look how beautiful the day

turned out after all, how in the distance the enemy
battalions are surrendering, and not a cloud in the sky—
what was I so worked up about? The villagers below
raise cattle, sheep, and goats; grow barley, wheat, flax,

and produce distinctive pottery. Pistachio nuts thrive
in the irrigated gardens of our city, as do pomegranates
naturally rich in antioxidants, which protect the body
from free radicals' interference with normal cell function.

Observation confirms that our chief building material
is mud brick left to bake in the sun, and with reason:
both mud and sun prove plentiful year-round, and the bricks
excel at keeping out the heat. A large harvest of reeds

drawn from one river to roof our houses also provides
long-lasting baskets, cradles, musical pipes, and the wedge-
shaped stylus with which we write on soft clay tablets.
The clay is taken from the other river. Writing comes from

our accountants. Hunting for food continues in the wetlands,
the forests, and the mountains, but in the walled cities
on the plains, it has become something more of a ritual
display of bravery, affluence, and the favor of the gods

who are the subjects of the greater part of all our artwork
along with warfare, mythic beasts, rulers, and palace life.
And yet here we find a fragment of glazed earthenware
depicting a simple mountain goat, and here a young archer

wears a headband, a richly decorated tunic, and fine sandals.
Such archers are known for shooting arrows backwards
and with great accuracy from the saddle, even at a gallop.
That figure of a winged bull with human face was given

a fifth leg to provide the creature with a sense of motion.
Our massive step pyramids—representative of mountains—
can be seen from a great distance across the flat landscape.
At the top of each pyramid rests a temple glazed in indigo

where the gods are known to dwell. Here is the river from which
we crawl, there the next into which we one day dissolve.
Music marks state occasions and serves to glorify the gods,
but the villagers enjoy non-ceremonial strains of it as well.

No one can be sure what sounds our instruments produce,
but we have theories about scales and tuning, astronomy,
mathematics, geography, which gems to wear to ward off
sickness and which to protect against thunderbolts and spirits.

When you see the king depicted balancing a basket of clay
effortlessly atop his tranquil head, this means it was he
who built our city's walls and many sparkling temples.
We have come into contact with other peoples through trade

and migration, but mostly warfare. If we are remembered
as cruel, ruthless warriors, were we not also scholars, restless
artists and lovers of art, obedient citizens, builders of cities
unmatched in magnificence, pious worshipers of the gods?

To the left and right of the city gate, a beneficent winged genie
holds a large pinecone used to sprinkle a blessing of water
on the heads of those who enter our city. Is it not reasonable
to suppose the same blessing is bestowed on those who leave?

CLAIR DE LUNE

↳ means "moonlight"

We revolt ourselves; we disgust and annoy us.
The way we look at us lately chills us to the core.
We become like those who seek to destroy us.

We push ourselves into small tasks that employ us
unrewardingly on purpose. We tire, we bore.
We revolt ourselves; we disgust and annoy us.

We rent ourselves to what force will enjoy us
into oblivion: wind, drink, sleep. We pimp, we whore.
We become like those who seek to destroy us.

We cat-and-mouse, roughhouse, inflatable-toy us
in our heads' red maze, in its den, on its shore.
We revolt ourselves; we disgust and annoy us.

We take offense at our being; we plot, we deploy us
against us and flummox; we wallow, we war.
We become like those who seek to destroy us.

If in triumph, our defeat; in torture, our joy is.
Some confusion so deep I can't fathom anymore.
We appall ourselves; we disgust and annoy us
into those we become we who seek to destroy us.

PARTIAL INVENTORY OF AIRBORNE DEBRIS

Small wonder I recoil
    even from my own
worn image looking back

where I always find it
    looking like it's trying
to warn me something

unspeakable is coming:
    Item. I stand before me
in a haze where people

can be made to want to
    make people stand
precariously on boxes,

arms wide open, strange
    hoods pulled down
over human faces, little live

wires hooked to various
      parts of the bodies
ridden on like donkeys,

smeared in feces, stacked
      one on top the other
for a photo to prolong

the swell an accomplishment
      like that engenders.
Item. What kept us from

discovering our selves'
      worst wasn't the lack
of evidence so much as

a failure of delivery, a kink
      overcome through
the push in technology

we've all had a hand in
      one way or the other.
Item. Looks like anyone

can be led as soon astray
      as to slaughter, disappearing
down the long ill-lit

institutional corridor
      misadventure unfolds
one synapse at a time—

and to presume immunity
  may be a symptom.
Item. In time I begin to

lose sensation, thoughts,
  I'm not complaining,
dropped a sedative in

tapwater and watched
  its demonstration on
what we have in common

with a sunset, gradual
  change and all the rest,
difficult to paraphrase

to be honest but I'm not
  complaining, it's like being
detained indefinitely

but with three meals a day
  on a tropical island!
Item. Looks like what's

done in my defense, or in
  its name, or in my
interest or in the image

of the same, no matter how
  distorted, fattened up
for laughs or plain dead-on,

connects to me by virtue
    of an invisible filament
over which I can claim

no know-how, no management,
    no muscle to speak of
(anatomical or spiritual),

what can I do, I can feel it
    tugging again, what have I
done: rotisserie chicken,

homestyle gravy, mac
    and cheese, a hot biscuit,
sweet potato casserole—

admit it, I'm on the fat side.
    Item. As when a putz
collapses to the dance hall's

floor and the pianist stops
    his performing mid–
waltz, always an angel

in a large brown gown
    bends over the slowly
reviving body and says

Don't stop Paul we need you
    now more than ever,
whereupon Paul, without

much thought, without
the burden of thinking,
sits back down, picks up

where he left off and plays.
Item. Or say a dream wolf
found my room by scent,

entered it, climbed upon
my sleeping throat
and camped there just to prove

its point, and when I woke
up I feared I'd never
save myself or even under-

stand what from without a little
alteration, meaning I
myself must somehow be

the wolf, and all the rest
must just be television.
Item. Only in the ion-

rich atmosphere around
a waterfall too immense
to be nostalgic did I feel

what I now know to be
"the feel of not to feel it."
Item. Actually I'm doing

imagination

much better now, maybe
    a little, what's the word,
soporose, I guess, I think

maybe I just needed to
    work it through and now
in its wake I feel a little

what was it again, a little
    soporose, that's right,
that captures it in a way

no other word could ever
    even hope to, I suppose,
I just feel soporose, so

soporose tonight, uniquely
    soporose. You think
I should be concerned?

FUN FOR
THE SHUT-IN

Demonstrate to yourself a resistance to feeling
unqualified despair by attempting something like
perfect despair embellished with hand gestures.

Redefine demonstration to include such movement as
an eye's orbit around the room; the pull of red
through drinking straws or the teeth of a comb;

random winces, twitches, tics; the winding of clocks
and tearing of pages; the neck hair's response
to uninvited sound, light, and the scent of oranges

where none in fact exist. Admit to yourself you lost
your absolute last goldfish, this one in a fashion
that looked more or less like relaxing, at least as you

have come to think it. There is an aspect of blue
seen only twice before: deep underwater, and now.
Take notice of the slow, practically imperceptible

changes always underway around or inside you like
tooth decay, apostasy, the accumulation of dust,
debt, the dead, and what the dead are preparing to say

if offered a seat at the table. Place the cold paperweight
toadlike on your forehead; hold inhumanly still.
Everyone comes close to growing their own avocado.

Everyone has a mind to plant it where they want to.
If you have power over breakfast, invest every burst
back into yourself to double the power at half the cost.

Messages from under the floorboards demand bed rest.
That handful of dried beans stitched into the sanctity
of twin paper plates makes the sound of never leaving

even brighter than before. Try amplifying the playback
from the rattle at hand to drown out any stubborn
thoughts to the contrary, the collapse of a country,

Steely Dan and the thunder of a hundred icebergs calving.
Offer the dead a seat at the table. Now take it away:
just pull it out from under them. Hypnosis is like deep

focus with a sleeper hold on self-critique. Attempt levitation
as a measure of your apology. Let's put it this way:
you don't want to be their bitch, but you don't want to

piss them off much, either. Ask them what they're having.
Listen with patience to their long elaborate talk.
Soon one of the dead will conduct an infinitely slow

white envelope across the unlit tabletop, a human sigh
through a wall of exhaust. The letter itself will be left
unsigned, but you'd recognize that handwriting anywhere.

CHIVAS REGAL

Right around here is where I start getting lost
in all the excitement of my right-hand glass

steadfast clinking down the long amble back
to the sofa where we sink in amber through the night.

Ghost messages in vibraphone, another double
neat, my head's mussed up but it's the only

source of heat and we crank it ever higher, aware
that even if we've cleared the air between us

ten thousand times before—you worry I worry
myself too much, I worry there isn't enough

you to last—whenever we do, we finish with a cup
of kindness down the hatch, with our selves

dissolving in short-lived blasts of old Aberdeen.
Here is a blindness to counter the clockwork

losses and a present too lived-in to cherish.
(Three Parliaments stubbed in a red glass plate

three longswords driven in a pictured heart in rain.)
Here is a liberty deep-kissing torpor, the lamp-

dust drifting in Sanskrit on my arm, my black-
bound notebook fallen hand to floor where

the bare foot is senseless to the serpent beneath it.
(Its glint eye watches me advance to the waters

and return converted to something tired, and poorer.)
In a less developed time, I would draw dragons

up from underground and score into their hide
the total histories of wind, but all there is at hand

tonight is troubled air, and upon this I inflict
what little marks I can before I lose again to sleep.

HIS EXCUSE

In the middle of your
speech I was over-

taken by the thought
that on an incline

north of here, the pine
in whose broad trunk

I will be buried was
toppled by a bobolink.

FANTASIES OF MANAGEMENT

When we tell ourselves
    that so many bells
have rung beyond
    our understanding,

what we really mean
    is that so many ring
counter to the way
    we wish to understand them.

When I think back
    long ago, almost back
to that barbaric time,
    what I want is to lie

down in a mile-wide
    bafflement of grasses
until there is nothing
    left of me but willingness

to go through it all
    again, because unless
a donut box of dollars
    falls down from the

sky I lie beneath admiring,
    it can't be avoided—
only this time, when they talk
    as if I have a choice

in the matter, a way to say
    no and live, I'll ask
if they wouldn't mind kindly
    doing me the favor

of repeating that please
    because I couldn't quite make out
whatever they just said
    through all that privilege.

THE CLOUD
CORPORATION

oppurtunity towards struggle

1

The clouds part revealing a mythology of clouds
assembled in light of earliest birds, an originary
text over water over time, and that without which

the clouds part revealing an apology for clouds
implicit in the air where the clouds had been
recently witnessed rehearsing departure, a heartfelt phrase

in the push of the airborne drops and crystals
over water over time—how being made to think
oneself an obstruction between the observer

and the object or objects under surveillance or even
desired—or if I am felt to be beside the point
then I have wanted that, but to block a path is like

not being immaterial enough, or being too much
when all they want from you now is your station
cleared of its personal effects please and vanish—

not that they'd ever just come out and say it when
all that darting around of the eyes, all that shaky
camouflage of paper could only portend the beginning of the

end of your tenure at this organization, and remember
a capacity to draw meaning out of such seeming
accidence landed one here to begin with, didn't it.

2

The clouds part revealing an anatomy of clouds
viewed from the midst of human speculation, a business
project undertaken in a bid to acquire and retain

control of the formation and movement of clouds.
As late afternoons I have witnessed the distant
towers borrow luster from a bourbon sun, in-box

empty, surround sound on, all my money made
in lieu of conversation—where conversation indicates
the presence of desire in the parties to embark on

exchange of spirit, hours forzando with heartfelt phrase—
made metaphor for it, the face on the clock tower
bright as a meteor, as if a torch were held against

likelihood to illuminate the time so I could watch
the calm silent progress of its hands from the luxury
appointments of my office suite, the tumult below

or behind me out of mind, had not my whole attention
been riveted by the human figure stood upon
the tower's topmost pinnacle, himself surveying

the clouds of the future parting in antiquity, a figure
not to be mistaken, tranquilly pacing a platform
with authority: the chief executive officer of clouds.

3

The clouds part revealing blueprints of the clouds
built in glass-front factories carved into cliff-faces
which, prior to the factories' recent construction,

provided dorms for clans of hamadryas baboons,
a species revered in ancient Egypt as attendants
of Thoth, god of wisdom, science, and measurement.

Fans conveying clouds through aluminum ducts
can be heard from up to a mile away, depending on
air temperature, humidity, the absence or presence

of any competing sound, its origin and its character.
It is no more impossible to grasp the baboon's
full significance in Egyptian religious symbolism

than it is to determine why clouds we manufacture
provoke in an audience more positive, lasting
response than do comparable clouds occurring in nature.

Even those who consider natural clouds products
of conscious manufacture seem to prefer that a merely
human mind lie behind the products they admire.

This development may be a form of self-exalting
or else another adaptation in order that we find
the hum of machinery comforting through darkness.

4

The clouds part revealing there's no place left to sit
myself down except for a single wingback chair
backed into a corner to face the window in which

the clouds part revealing the insouciance of clouds
cavorting over the backs of the people in the field
who cut the ripened barley, who gather it in sheaves,

who beat grain from the sheaves with wooden flails,
who shake it loose from the scaly husk around it,
who throw the now threshed grain up into the gently

palm-fanned air whose steady current carries off
the chaff as the grain falls to the floor, who collect
the grain from the floor painstakingly to grind it

into flour, who bake the flour into loaves the priest will offer
in the sanctuary, its walls washed white like milk.
To perform it repeatedly, to perform it each time

as if the first, to walk the dim corridor believing that
the conference it leads to might change everything,
to adhere to a possibility of reward, of betterment,

of moving above, with effort, the condition into which
one has been born, to whom do I owe the pleasure
of the hum to which I have been listening too long.

5

The clouds part revealing the advocates of clouds,
believers in people, ideas and things, the workers
of the united fields of clouds, supporters of the wars

to keep clouds safe, the devotees of heartfelt phrase
and belief you can change with water over time.
It is the habit of a settled population to give ear to

whatever is desirable will come to pass, a caressing
confidence—but one unfortunately not borne out
by human experience, for most things people desire

have been desired ardently for thousands of years
and observe—they are no closer to realization today
than in Ramses' time. Nor is there cause to believe

they will lose their coyness on some near tomorrow.
Attempts to speed them on have been undertaken
from the beginning; plans to force them overnight

are in copious, antagonistic operation today, and yet
they have thoroughly eluded us, and chances are
they will continue to elude us until the clouds part

in a flash of autonomous, ardent, local brainwork—
but when the clouds start to knit back together again,
we'll dismiss the event as a glitch in transmission.

6

The clouds part revealing a congregation of bodies
united into one immaterial body, a fictive person
around whom the air is blurred with money, force

from which much harm will come, to whom my welfare
matters nothing. I sense without turning the light
from their wings, their eyes; they preen themselves

on the fire escape, the windowsill, their pink feet
vulnerable—a mistake to think of them that way.
If I turn around, the room might not be full of wings

capable of acting, in many respects, as a single being,
which is to say that I myself may be the source of
what I sense, but am no less powerless to change it.

Always around me, on my body, in my mouth, I fear them
and their love of money, everything I do without
thinking to help them make it. And if I am felt to be

beside the point, I have wanted that, to live apart
from what depends on killing me a little bit to keep
itself alive, and yet not happily, with all its needs

and comforts met, but fattened so far past that point
I am engrossed, and if I picture myself outside of it
it isn't me anymore, but a parasite cast out, inviable.

7

The clouds part revealing the distinction between
words without meaning and meaning without words,
a phenomenon of nature, the westbound field

of low air pressure developing over water over time
and warm, saturated air on the sea surface rising
steadily replaced by cold air from above, the cycle

repeating, the warm moving upward into massive
thunderclouds, the cold descending into the eye
around which bands of thunderclouds spiral, counter-

clockwise, often in the hundreds, the atmospheric
pressure dropping even further, making winds
accelerate, the clouds revolve, a confusion of energy,

an incomprehensible volume of rain—I remember
the trick of thinking through infinity, a crowd of eyes
against an asphalt wall, my vision of it scrolling

left as the crowd thinned out to a spatter and then
just black until I fall asleep and then just black again,
past marketing, past focus groups, past human

resources, past management, past personal effects,
their insignificance evident in the eye of the dream
and through much of the debriefing I wake into next.

2

THE NIGHT SHIP

Roll back the stone from the sepulcher's mouth!
I sense disturbance deep within, as if some sorcery

had shocked the occupant's hand alive again, back
to compose a document in calligraphy so dragonish

that a single misstep made it necessary to stop
right then and there and tear the botched draft up,

begin again and stop, tear up again and scatter
a squall of paper lozenges atop the architecture

that the mind designs around it, assembling a city
somewhat resembling the seaport of your birth,

that blinking arrangement of towers and signage
you now wander underneath, drawn by the spell

of the sea's one scent, by the bell of the night ship
that cleaves through the mist on its path to the pier.

Surrender to that vision and the labor apprehensible
as you take to the streets from the refuge of a chair

so emphatically comfortable even Lazarus himself
would have chosen to remain unrisen from its velvet,

baffling the messiah, His many onlookers awkwardly
muttering to themselves, downcast till a sudden

dust devil spirals in from the dunes—a perfect excuse
to duck back indoors. (Sand spangles their eyes;

the little airborne stones impinge upon such faces
as only Sorrow's pencil would ever dare to sketch,

and even then, it wouldn't be a cakewalk, you realize.
The dust devil at sea would recall a waterspout.)

You fear that you have been demanded into being
only to be dropped on the wintry streets of this

imagination rashly, left easy prey for the dockside
phantoms, unwatched and unawaited, and I know

what you mean, almost exactly. This cardboard city
collapses around us; another beautiful document

disassembles into anguish (a cymbal-clap) and we can't
prevent it. At one the wind rises, and the night ship

trembles, drowsing back into its silver cloud. At two it embarks
upon a fiercer derangement. We are in this together.

And we will find protection only on the night ship.

CHAPTER
FOR BEING
TRANSFORMED
INTO A
SPARROW

1

The world tries hard to bore me to death, but not hard enough.
Today it made me sit immobile in the bath-
water upwards of an hour, but the fact is, World—

I was totally into it. There's a canker anchored
at the root of everything. Even I know that. Now what I want
is to know it better, want to know deep down

I can return to the world whatever filth I receive
without compunction. I knew humility once
and she died on the floor. What power do you think

you have over me? Even fastened in your turning
tepid and beyond, what I felt was strengthened,
downright strong. The end comes once, I said, then what—

What carries me now? A sudden heartwave
moving rapidly, increasing with a pinch of recollected incense.
Steady, spirit. We will address our Dead:

—What are you now, a whisper? A vapor minnow
in the rue-blue seize that never loosens, not even

for a minute, not for a half-lived something
like a dream? I trust the eloquent have already

tried opening that grip with flattery and failed; possibly
the only currency to grease a palm that monstrous

has to be the same old prank of paper we have here—
or don't have, cheerfully (not quite cheerfully).

See what can be bartered, what sacrifice's smoke
appeases over others': there is nothing beneath me.

2

There is nothing beneath me: the days keep coming
as if significant: events strain the heavenly, weak-
seamed sack in which they're pent; when one slips through,

kaboom! that's history, and I am nothing better
than a shattered passenger, I pass by. Pictures develop
more speedily than ever, in an hour if you ask.

Remember the one of us on the ocean, salt-wincing
on the two-tone flotation device? I can't take it anymore,
photography. How it flattens memory's body down

to a roll of surfaces—insistent surfaces; persuasive, yes,
but not convincing, though they threaten everywhere
to take the place of, usurping what they'd save, the way

a javelin of lavender, sprung from the close of a once-
loved book, asserts a dozen verities: first that of the plant
from which it came, then of its having been removed

(and that by human hand), then of a time, however measured
(and that for waving through a field), next of the soil
from which it grew, and by extension, of the world—

inclusive of the book, and of the time, and even
of the hand—but never how it felt, what anxiety or rapture
conducted or conducts it, what faith in what ability

of anything to capture, what brought it to begin with,
what labor of the blood, what accident of lavender
dismantled now on carpet, what measure of the spirit

and of its having been removed, which is perhaps
now waving through a field, and that from which it grew:
keep waving through that field, keep waiting, please.

3

After the first weeks after, I lost myself remembering
the worth of what was lost, the cost of which was nothing.
Between myself and where I stood, there fell a distance

only loss could fill, an empty world, a simpleness, its shadows
thrown across my window. Often the mind would try
to stay itself by imagining: a falling through the many

numbered levels of the air, each level its progressively
thinner shade of blue, as if the air nearest earth
were the least of its forms, or had been ruined by what happens.

And always as it fell the mind would snag upon a saving
branch before colliding with the planet beneath it.
No small debate surrounded the origin of that branch:

had the mind itself devised it, or had you put it there?
Its significance, however, was certain: something in the mind
clearly warranted protecting, but what remained unclear.

4

In the shade of the need to know, to know that what was once
remains, grows the knowledge that what was

was almost certainly not that, not merely,
not once. There is a way through all of this—

a ladder, yes—but it's a ladder made of thread.
In the shade of the need, keep waiting, please.

A day or two before they tore the pall of ivy
down from the wall that held the hill in place,

the invisible sparrows that had made of it a shelter
seemed to sing a little differently, sing a little

less, as if in apprehension, and what happened to them
keeps happening to me. My green retreat

has folded, drawn into itself without me
in it, and had I known that it would, there

would be less repeating now, or as much, but
softer. At the barren wall, where what has been

has been erased, the only phrase I stand
with loving to remember, with temper I perpetuate:

5

who had pictured the world as one of degrees, from root
to stalk, from stalk to flower, from flower to breath

has learned to suffocate at last, and will not be found
recumbent on the davenport, trawling the creases

for sweetmeats past and the fruits of human reason.
When I open the door to perceive you—you are there.

Stay, illusion. There are so many things. Be with me
on Harlem Meer, where you can be alligator

grown past keeping. On with me to Gorman Park, where
"stairs slant down into the dark / declivity of ivy

wind and fallen / brown, late afternoon a weathered book"
from which I will never leave, not breathing. Broken

vessel, broken thought: late afternoon in Gorman Park, be with me
that in what leaves will breathe in what is broken.

You were the sparrow in the laundromat. I trapped you
in the whelm of a pillowcase, showed you to the street

with human decency, care. You looked me back into
myself. And as then, so now—I commend you to the air.

TO HIS OWN DEVICE

That figure in the cellarage you hear upsetting boxes
is an antic of the mind, a baroque imp cobbled
up under bulbs whose flickering perplexes night's

impecunious craftsman, making what he makes
turn out irregular, awry, every effort botched
in its own wrong way. You belong, I said, laid out chalk-

white between a layer of tautened cotton gauze
and another of the selfsame rubbish that you are
wreaking havoc on tonight—and it didn't disagree.

What's more, I said, you are amiss in this ad hoc quest
for origin and purpose. Whatever destiny it is
you are meant to aspire to before you retire to

that soup-bowl of oblivion such figments as we
expect to find final rest in couldn't possibly be
contained in these boxes. And again—no contest.

And when I was in need, I said, you raveled off
in the long-winded ploys of a winless October,
unfaithful to the one whose instincts had devised you . . .

—At this, the figure dropped the box from its hands,
turned down a dock I remembered and wept.
I followed it down there, sat beside it and wept.

Looking out on the water in time we came to see
being itself had made things fall apart this way.
We envied the simplicity implicit in sea-sponges

and similar marine life, their resistance to changes
across millennia we took to be deliberate, an art
practiced untheatrically beneath the water's surface.

We admired the example the whole sea set, actually.
Maritime pauses flew like gulls in our exchanges.
We wondered that much longer before we had left.

CHAPTER
FOR BREATHING
AIR AMONG
THE WATERS

Whereat the one clear thought
    I might ride on the remainder
of my wakefulness was taken

    by the throat and carried under

the surface leaving me
                not freed
    but caught up in what thinking
tries to conceal:
            its foundation
    made of clouds, an anchorage

in sinking down where to know
    is to feel knowledge dissolving
into particles of pause, the many

    stoppages and starts that shape
by sounding each possible maze

through a landscape of otherwise
perfectly nothing.
                    I could lie here

on the ocean's floor, not human
anymore, picked clean of it, long

after the last petition for rescue
tears through the darkening film

overhead.
                    After ages of strange

susurrations plait into a dubious
        prophecy.
                    After the ghost of me
snags in the verbiage of rust-blue
        weeds and fades.
                    But as the deep

dislodges us in parcels, slow time
        reassembles: hands hard to clamp

open, limbs barnacled; the tongue
        eeling ahead through whatever

idiom it needs.
                    If oceanic winter
battens us on absences, shadows,

on palpable blankness,

           as ancient
   waters heat, we take on velocity.

And when, unsleeving, grown large
   in their confinement, the rebel
tentacles drive us
         toward daylight,
   then we, oblivious, blinking, emerge.

THE LAST DREAM OF LIGHT RELEASED FROM SEAPORTS

And such proceedings shall be considered criminal:
amusement amendments, two or more individuals,
any dream proceedings which engage in the activities

indicating intention, love, or other things of value;
a safe house, a biological boulevard, communications
that demonstrate the actor plans to commit rips

in new material, transfer funds, have everlasting vision.
Wendy, a sadness shall take effect on the specified
streets until the real is removed together with the findings.

If removal is unlikely, they shall take the sentence,
the beach facilities, and the foreseeable future into custody
and charge all with a criminal offense not later than

seven days after the commencement of such strap
from physical officers, offenses to the hide, such striking
dismantling electronic surveillance, wild highway!

The broken may be released on a table of contents,
except in the circuit where hands are provided,
mandatory madness, or the enactment of documents

along the northern border, where huddled personnel
trap adequate undercurrent, make criminal history,
and waive such intelligence as necessary for the purpose

of transcending platforms with certain maritime girls
during dangerous velvet, beyond wrecking trains,
beyond staff plastic and the sudden injury to buildings

provided for the placement, the procedures for taking
the liberty of fingerprints, chrome updates of extracts,
a lookout for persons seeking to confirm a cost-effective kiss

fully integrated to soul points and a privacy database.
Wendy, carry out provisions to limit the authority
upon terms consistent with the feasibility of enhancing

clandestine telephone matter, the length of service,
and small activities protected by the united light of mirrors.
Headquarters are in the field the first night it appears

in such mist as issued under the jurisdiction of harbors.
Acts dangerous to human life occur primarily within.
Any person who conceals in good faith has legs to believe

in domestic possession, a likely subject, the written scream
that produces new agency, a consistent sweat paragraph.
Center the lonely secretary in accordance with such guidelines

as defined by the dream engines, or by striking the engines
and inserting machines, a firearm, the town weapon,
or other device found on wanted tramps of prominence

who pose known threat to the amended bones of heroes
and higher education. This development is amended
each place it appears. Each place it is amended, it appears

again, appointing frauds of rearview, affecting deputy
and primary duties, committing unauthorized camera sadness,
counterintelligence, false access to disclosure mansions,

sprung local liquid, acts of text assault, and distinct verbal gas.
Wendy, stand in the wake of events, stand resolutely
vibrant in the worship of the possible, the fullest human hands.

New obstacles shall be established by the chairman of failure.
Authorized language drones shall implement and expand
written combat, chance procedures, and the day period, while the night

force shall determine public and personal want and want-
removal with a program of general sense regulations, preventing
any means of notice, including but not limited to the light

released from seaports, suicide, and the individual dream.

BLED

Thereafter it happened there would be no future
arrangements made as the present had begun
handing itself over to the past with such vehemence
whatever happened already happened before
or stopped its happening the moment it began.
To look forward meant looking in where you stood
astonished to be looking behind you instead
into the distance where the water's surface split
and spread to a pane of undisturbed waters.
Arguments among half-thoughts could continue
then as now and did, scattering particles
of gray on more gray, an expanse pinned down
at the corners but taught by a sea-wind to shudder
nonstop. To stand an oculus among that sea's
gray arrangements meant scattering half-
thoughts to such astonishment that whatever
began to happen split, spread, and handed itself
over to a past where having happened meant more
being stopped. To look with vehemence
disturbed the water's surface as arguments
wind made of the future now shuddered
distantly behind you. To look forward back into
the expanse of such waters meant to want
momentarily not to continue, seeing as to continue
meant what it did, but thereafter already
even to want that bled to no particular gray.

DISPATCH FROM BEHIND THE MOUNTAIN

[handwritten annotations:]

• line sentence → extension of the breath
• imagery
• diction
↳ end-stop
• completed thought
• concentrated pause
- enjamed
- transition
- momentary fictions

↳ I thought this title would be more about mountains

Then there's this: a page
torn from the original
stupor to which the mind
is always driven to
return, drawn by a calling
back to the memory

- colon
- "a page torn"
enjambed lines
→ single sentence poem

♡

of what must have been a room
you abandoned
impulsively, caught up
in the fluster of a vast
misunderstanding, or else
a room you never left

interesting break in stanza
(concentrated pause)

1 Sentence = 1 thought
- relates to his Apologia on (page 88)
↳ poem about thought

without the sense you were leaving
something of value
puzzled in the billows
pulsing underwater—
and even as you turn
to retrieve what's lost

♡ 3

leaving
- search for meaning
- sense of rooms
↳ maybe rooms of thought within the mind like chambers opening and closing

• Donnelly uses a lot of abstract words
• Stupor—trance, near unconsciousness
• thinks often about negative mind spaces and tries to talk about it

57

you know you never will
   except in pieces, random
glimpses of a nothing
   you want only to possess
     again entirely, entirely
   without sacrifice, as if

   to sift living long enough
     among dim lamps
might press into your hands
     the sum of all the pages
     missing or else leave you
     briefly able to compose

an apparatus which might
    force the infinite back into the cabin
of your thought now and stop
    the animals where they drink
     along the perimeter
    of the lake beneath your sleep.

[handwritten annotations:]

"sacrifice"

?

apparatus: the technical equiptment or machinery

dream? where did animals come from

what is the point of writing in negative language and use words that are hard to understand, yet beautiful?

NO DIARY

minutes are hours in the noctuary of terror,—terror has no diary
CHARLES MATURIN

Through the chinks of the trap door / what we call life
presents itself as a kind of task, namely that of acquiring

amid all the horrors / more of itself, but as this task is
undertaken, stepping out from its shadow, there appears

a few minutes later / another, more difficult task, namely
that of distracting one's thoughts from the burden of

at every moment / that which one has striven to acquire.
That some grave mistake, inoperable, nests in the cog-

as I entered the church / work of that life proves abundantly
clear: through a chambered air, a convergence of needs

while I uttered these words / hard to satisfy, whose short-
lived satisfaction achieves no more than a pause in the

midnight / noise devolving in time into a boredom that is
at once beachfront property and proof of the emptiness

at last / of existence per se. If existence held intrinsic
positive value, then there would be nothing left to refer to

as I set the lamp down / as boredom: it would be enough
merely to exist. But mischance cut the power without

the clock struck two / which we are powerless: moonlight
confuses us with its statuary: we find nothing adequate

while I poured out my heart / to strive after or fear that
doesn't disappoint. Little wonder then we should cast

into the garden / hours into distance, difficulties, gambits
designed to perpetuate the illusion that our goal might

with dropt and wordless lips / satisfy. Intellectual activity
removes us briefly from the swelter of existence. This is

the clock struck three / its interest. Any sensual pleasure
fades on attaining its object. We know when we are not

on the verge of extinction / lost in such pursuits, thoughts
lilt back to the terms of this existence, its fundamental

feeling my fear about to be / insignificance, leaving one
furious with it, but protective nonetheless, as one might lay

in a fever / one's hands in tenderness upon the heaving
animal one is given to destroy, even though I have come

over and over / through long experiment to abhor being
nothing terrifies me more than the prospect of it stopped.

EPITAPH
BY HIS
OWN HAND

From the morning he started
    peeling his first potato

he felt like he'd been peeling
    potatoes for eternity—

all that fell about his ankles
    like clouds' inky shadows

smudged across the pastures
    of an afterlife clearly

put farther away from him
    the harder he worked for it.

POEM BEGINNING WITH A SENTENCE FROM *THE MONK*

Far from growing familiar with my prison
    I beheld it every moment with new horror.
Thoughts to which a mind should not be driven
    drove me through a bank of devilment in flower.

Thoughts to which the mind had grown immune
    soon sickened me against me, turned me
in among me stranger than before, my quarantine a panic
    room bricked in, a tightening around me

in increments only animals know. And now I inch
    the walls like ivy, probing the brickwork
with patient cheek for cracks admitting outside air.
    And now I feel, or feel I hear, a livid spark

through an old antenna on the tower's top. And now
    I wish what others spoke were stilled inside
the mind in stoppered, mouth-blown bottles,
    and I'd place these bottles in cabinets made

to resemble faces, and what was said would stay
    where you'd expect to find it: in the cabinet
pertaining to the face of the person who had said it.
    It may or may not be necessary to point out

this isn't the first I've been seized by the thought.
    I have in the past found pleasant distraction
assembling a taskforce to distill speech data, another
    to oversee its placement in cabinets, a third

to tend to the general upkeep, a last to awaken me
    with a mild ringing: I have the gong already.
Storage of this nature should, but can't, be infinite—
    one's archive's blueprints echo one's anatomy.

Something mere about the word brides my crazy.
    It may or may not be necessary to point out
it could be said, to revise a statement made above,
    I feel a strange degree of familiar discomfort,

as if the closeness of my skin went atmospheric, aglow
    with insignificant warmth, as when a flashlight
lights the mouth, or burning hot, as when Pazuzu
    visits from the south, bearing storms and fever.

What interests me is forever can't tell a difference
        without dissolving it. If certain cheerfulness
comes with the territory, apparently some sacrifice
        does too, but it's a kind that goes unnoticed.

Standing before the cabinet of your face, I unstop
        a bottle; I savor its phrase's nuances. And although
you are far from this undertaking, you are closing in
        in spirit. And although I have often felt buried alive

like an architect in the tomb it was his dumb luck to design
        for a paranoid king, looking around here as if
I were its visitor, really taking it in on its own terms
        and not just paying lip service to the big idea,

doing the work of putting words to the way I feel
        in the thick of it, a little like building a birdhouse
underwater, I see no reason why, given a modest
        number of revisions, I couldn't grow to love it.

HIS AGENDA

All these empty pages must correspond to the days
devoted to lying in the bygone style, the head

buoyed for hours in a harbor of jade pillows, eyes
turned to the window where the hours bled from blue

to deeper blue then burned away—the whole day
dazzled into night without innovation, the sky again

the temple of the mind perceiving it, the clouds
becoming thoughts like pilgrims chance had carried there.

I think of them arriving in the bygone style, in light-
colored robes and lamblike manner, their simple

fluctuations visible through the linden branches
that would not have been in leaf or flower at the time.

I think of him attentive to the pilgrim voices, softest
silver audible to inmost ear, and also of the pleasure

that he must have taken there, a pleasure I admire
somewhat more than I admit, and put the shut book down.

THE RUMORED
EXISTENCE
OF OTHER
PEOPLE

I dreamt my household consisted largely of objects
manufactured by people I would never meet or know
and some of these objects dangled down from the ceiling
while others towered dizzily upwards from the floor.

If most of them stayed where I left them as if dozing
in embryonic thought, still others came with features
conducive to movement, making them appear more
endearingly alive as they powered up and off in search

of excitement, an hour's diversion—no harm in that.
Intuition stopped short of determining whether or not
any of the objects kept in contact with their makers
via some kind of bond, perhaps a physical connection

explicable through science, or else a spiritual affinity
notoriously difficult for an outside party to understand.
But the more I gave it thought the more it seemed to me
believable. A silver line, a souvenir, a sieve of relation

meaning to release something lovingly means always
remaining tied to it. As to be somewhere completely
means never having to leave. I thought to figure out how
many presences collected around me at that moment.

Did they possess consciousness, would they cooperate.
Should I expect a new kind or the mundane damages.
Everywhere I might be now in light of where I've been.
I dreamt I held out my hand and before long a banana

flew up from the industrious parenthesis of Costa Rica
and provided for that hand before it knew it wanted.
Start slow, be consistent, and your levels will increase.
I dreamt the will of manufacturers to produce goods

was shed from those goods long after they were made.
All the windows overlooking a landfill or production site.
The more I gave it thought the more it seemed to me
obvious. Also touching. Whoever built that warehouse

across the way built it thinking someone would one day
look at it in wonder. Also sorrow. To keep an endless
store of that feeling. To make, to provide it. That I might
turn my back on a building like that will have become

unthinkable tomorrow, when my sympathy with most
abandoned things is effectively cut from the budget.
I dreamt in increments of three, five, and eventually ten.
Not the way the objects at hand rubbed me but more

the way those beyond me made me pang for them there.
I might even say the walls, the floors, the plush carpets
unrolled on the floors and the furniture, the refrigerator
and any item in it, nautical tchotchkes and the curtains

clamped tight as August quahogs to optimize my output.
The shedding of the will, too, takes place incrementally
across decades, late at night, the little shifting in a room's
air profile comparable to a ghost's entrance if not quite

equivalent. At work beyond the warehouse, everything
else: droplets on navy felt, protection sensed in a system
whose products had begun to forecast accurate wants.
I dreamt a body's indentation beside me on the mattress

vanishing as the presence found the door through a film
adaptation of silence. Child with gifts for ravens in pockets.
Lady affianced to alien abduction. Figure of the human
experiment almost over. I open my mouth and in no time

lasagna, Chianti, a greater than expected rate of melting,
atrophy, military action, and a ravenousness that shook
my confidence and the hinged box I keep pin money in.
The rumble of it recalls the convulsion Plato says the gods

sank Atlantis with to chasten its inhabitants, whose vast
majority descended from Poseidon and one of the island's
earth-born shepherdesses. As long as divinity remained
predominant in their nature, Atlanteans kept obedient to

the laws of their progenitor, but over time, what was divine
diminished, and love of wisdom and virtue gave way to
love of wealth and luxury, which in the past had seemed
merely distractions. To those who lacked the ability to see

through the radiance of things, the Atlanteans appeared
to be thriving: palaces, baths, mines rich in orichalcum.
Herds of elephants. Vineyards, orchards. Access to upwards
of a dozen sherbets. The chance to astonish houseguests

with golden oblongs and lozenges. To watch as vampires
turned mortals into vampires for cash, despite the fact
that vampires could easily devise a life without having to
dirty their pale hands with money again, but apparently

nothing restores that old vitality like a night of spending.
I dreamt a percentage of my money had been touched
by entrepreneurs of the undead. I dreamt I'd never guess
how much. Dreamt no idea where my money had been.

What bathroom floor or choir stall or Alp or what disgrace.
Dreamt I couldn't taste a difference. Dreamt my money
might want company, and I had better not keep putting it
in my mouth in that case. As drawing from a songbird's

coloratura, I dreamt the secret to prosperity is being
commonesque. Profiteroles, remote control, the ruin of
my body. And tremulous as horses hidden in old plaster.
Confused as vinyl siding. Certain as what's happening

can't have all at once, or even all that fast, but by degrees
imperceptible until too late, eyes trained to other tasks
as the sheep took to clover, distracted as a vortex of plastic
debris measuring twice the size of Texas patched itself

together mid-Pacific, a swirl like a god's intoxicated eye
but not surveillant, voyeuristic, a bright new continent
only in it for the kicks, its culture to bask, its historiography
accidental, with every bit of flotsam serving as a double

record of one product's manufacture and consumption.
I dreamt in complex packaging that posed no less a threat
at the factory warehouse than up among my cupboards
or dropped in the superabundant trash bins at airports.

Found it simple and good to forget that threat by letting
perception of such objects eclipse true knowledge of them.
Any worry washed in umbra. Like being in the moment
only endlessly. I hear the naked hands of strangers make

my dumplings but experience insists what makes them
mine is money. I open the door and I extend good money
into ancient night, night prosperous with stars, order heavy
in my hand. I'm immortal that way. I lie down and I feed.

3

NO MISSION STATEMENT, NO STRATEGIC PLAN

When loathing's narwhal thrusts its little tusk
 deep into the not-for-profit of my thought
and anchors in the planks across which I have

stomped unfathomable hours, and thanklessly;
 when I feel the panic of it struggling to dislodge
and all the damage done to the ship thereby—

the prow, to be exact, if we agree this is a ship,
 and now I fear we have no choice—when lost
in drear blue Baffin Bay, if night's first voice

says *Quick, we're sinking, yank that narwhal out*,
 it must be night's second, less impetuous voice
saying *Not so fast. Why not leave it where it is?*

THE NEW
HISTRIONICISM

When the actor on stage slams his fist against the table
one last time, his other hand holding a worry-heavy brow,
half-shadowing his eyes, we can almost taste the thumb
of circumstance bearing down on him, and we know what now
he has to become: a man of action, opponent to the forces
that brought him to this crisis. We'll watch as he chooses

his moves with caution, demonstrating as never before
what we have come to call free will, his plight felt so acutely
we have no choice but to believe in it, even if we know
that the path our hero manages to cut through the hedge
maze of opposition was actually penned forth centuries ago
in the looping longhand of an author now conveniently

apart from the drama which seems to reveal the illusory
nature of free will even as it attempts to excite our faith in it.
All my life, I thought to myself, asking for the tremendous
embarrassment it drew up in me and against which I fought
whole- to half-heartedly, making of my mind a religious
rite observed by no one but me and my understudy, static

windowside as cloud shadows advance over ancient pastures
monks tend sheep in. I send my latest bulletin their way
by way of thought but it can't be made out above the fuss
gathering in the herb garden as, true to form, a massive ship
flying head-to-wind, sails luffing, cuts through the chill air-
waves raveling upward from the mouths of distant heather.

I signal to the monks again, only this time via semaphore,
as in ship to shore, but they're still too distracted to notice.
Meanwhile the hero places his hands palm-down on the table.
He pushes his chair back, starts to rise. Then the house goes
black, pitching us into the dark at this—the decisive moment.
A struggle between the darkness and the sense I control it

ends abruptly. The darkness is not nice. The ship steadily
approaches the monastery as if sailing on the surface of the sea.
When the lights come back up, the hero reappears, pacing
across the ship's deck's planks in what we have come to call
anxiety. I drop my typewriter out the window to show I know
what is expected. That the hero and the others on board

will notice monks pacing on the earth below them and drop
anchor right then and there. It lands in the bed of lavender.
Monks crowd around the anchor and seize it as if their own,
though the rule states clearly that none shall receive a message
or a gift without first informing the abbot, and that even if
the abbot knows and orders the article to be accepted, it lies

within his power to present it to whichever brother he chooses.
Moreover the brother for whom an article was intended
mustn't grow angry, inward or upset should it find its way
into another's hands, as such behavior only serves to present
the devil with an opportunity. As the air takes on the scent
of crushed communal lavender, in the darkness comes a voice

that says that it belongs to me. It comes to test one's mettle.
Meanwhile the hero, red with the monks' untoward behavior,
leaps overboard to reclaim the anchor, moving deliberately
downward through the air through what we have come to call
swimming. Though the rule states clearly that every guest
must be greeted with courtesy, with heads bowed in utmost

humility and care, the arrival of a ship by way of air proves
no less incompatible with convention than a sense of urgency
proves palpable even from my parapet. But it's impossible
to tell if, when the monks grab our hero, they do so in rowdy
welcome, or to pry him away from the too-prized anchor, or away
from the miracle they've mistaken for the devil's snare. *Stop*,

he says as they drag him to the earth, *you are drowning me.*
Again, amid struggle: *You are drowning me.* Then kill the lights.
Centuries afterwards, visiting the site where these events
came to pass, walking the grounds, I think what I remember
most is a feeling of being apart from them, the great loneliness
which seems to be one's lesson. In the herb garden, I look up

and realize the window I sat at wasn't far away at all. I think
they were all just ignoring me, or angry at me for making them
self-conscious about what they were trying to sleep through.
As I leave the theater, its unlit halls wind in no direction I can see.
Then I see there are no halls, it's all just one big empty space.
Then, in the darkness, the voice again. And it says I control this.

MONTEZUMA TO HIS MAGICIANS

If they are gods, if they have
divinity in them, then why

when we lay at their feet
garlands of quetzal feathers

and gold coins do they leap
upon the gold as dazzled

monkeys might and tread
on sacred plumage like dust?

DREAM OF ARABIAN HILLBILLIES

Salutations from the all-encompassing
    arms of a hammered millionaire!
I send a blessing of watches over your body
    and a messenger to your folks

sanctifying them in a long crude eruption.
    May you journey in the security
of a huge American truck. May your enemies come
    to wither in front of this truck

allowing you and your kinfolk to occupy
    the avenue of personal interests
privately and in full style for 60,000 years.
    Talk about divine measures!

All enemy forces threatening your basic
    philosophy of life demand a helpin'
of grievous medicine: it is no longer possible
    to press letters of forgiveness

loaded with soft words and in diplomatic
    style into their hands when clearly
in their hearts they would strip you of such
    incredible resources: money out

back in important places, a wicked grip
    on the situation, pools of lost time
and no little grace ... but who can push the enemy
    underground with hospitality?

No one. Gain control of circumstances by
    taking some. Repel with mischief
raised to the utmost power, one forbidden
    behavior after another, from pure

dissociation from the feelings and prides
    of your forefathers to aggression
against the infrastructures of the sea and sky.
    Spell serious danger to their being,

y'all—only half your hoard is remaining.
    I address you now with a big torch
of guidance handed over to me by the stars
    above Texas. It is unacceptable

to assist the enemy in your dispossession.
    Be not bitten by the same snake
twice. The first explosion inspired
    the devil, and the second a gathering

of military leaders who talk to you through such
    fast-moving light, one day today
is tomorrow's fear commercial, thank you
    very much. The money you pay

out for loving this world will all come back
    for the money you have left, saying
"To express hate and anger is a moral gesture
    to the future." I did *not* just say that.

Time to be enshrined in the sanctities
    of pleasure, not dragged through the streets
of the bubblin' in your head that is
    the persistence of news agencies.

Time to liberate that head from the whole
    world's behind and listen for a pen
to spell the words of your foes' humiliation.
    Why not paradise before as well as

after death, kept at a beautiful 72 degrees
    and with nothing between you
and all the privileges heapin' so high
    a neck is pinched just signing up for them?

Terrorizing the snake for twisting filthy
    text to your house is a human duty.
Let your good black shoes witness you push
    hard into the red dust of the battle

burning your intestines like a pagan tea.
    Cleanse the road to your destiny
of all idolaters and claim what they be droppin'
    for your booty. Take no captives—

or maybe one or two, should they surrender
    wealth, drink, hearts and selves
to your supremacy without hesitation.
    Paradise's nearness isn't getting any

better. May you not cave in and weep deep. May wolves
    not eat your wings. May your life
not be a lifelong movie of your life
    but a steadfast becoming other than that

which you are: a slave to the power
    fiddling among hills of fed clouds and shaken
into wonderment like a shot horse barely
    gathering will to lay down with it, y'hear?

CHAPTER FOR BEING TRANSFORMED INTO A LOTUS

The comparison only went so far: the suffering
from which we had come to expect so much
remained mere suffering; the swamp due south

to which we had thought to compare it in our youth
stayed water choked in excess life, its voices
thoughtlessly forcing the same plump syllables

across the distance into windows furred with night.
But here in the room where we sit thinking that
if suffering had to enter our house, it should have

been the kind that sang, or else the kind from which
small shapes would zoom and circle the light
hanging in the middle of the room like a thought

whose fifteen petals open and whose opening we become
custodian to, here in the lotus of half-sleep, I am
beginning to forget where a comparison falls short.

ANTEPENULTIMATE
CONFLICT
WITH SELF

1

The times the thought of being pulled apart from
you comes as a relief have come now to outnumber
those it startles me like light from a hurricane
lamp left burning unattended dangerously near
the curtains of the theater we both attend and are.

The fire of it spasms up the tall glass chimney
like little air pockets we've watched trudge down
loops in hospital tubing—disarmed, but quietly.
When I have made in our manhood some large noise
to spook off harm, harm has only found us faster.

Saying one should distract it as the other escapes
to an agreed-on spot where we can reconnoiter
after, like under the alder where the jackdaw builds
its nest of surplus playbills. They shred them up
like that as a matter of procedure. They intend no

particular disrespect to you or your production.
None taken. Glad to hear it. Because I thought I saw
a darkness drift across your face that I associate
with umbrage. Not even close. If I were you I wouldn't
flatter myself. And yet, turning things around, this

darkness you speak of, it must have drifted across
your own face at least as much as mine. Admittedly, yes.
So why not leave me out of it? I've been trying to do
just that. Looks to me like you haven't been going
about it right. That makes two of us, then. Not quite.

Leaving the burning theater behind one begins to
ease into a new perspective. The stairway leads to
a doorway, the doorway to an alleyway, the alleyway
to another door, more stairs, another amber room
where one can forget again, its window overlooking

a car lot emptied of its cars. The stark lines recall
what was and will be there, but isn't now or anymore.
The scent of juniper or cat piss. A knock at the door.
A look around the room before opening to confirm this
isn't the one we've been, only half in fear, dreaming.

2

After calculation, I've let you in. Seated at the table
in cold beneath the window, we try to remember each
example of the condition we're after, namely that of
a multitude at work in unison. You say alder branches
blown in the wind. I say the warp and weft of waves

on an open bay. You say activity near beehives. I say
heavy snowfall. You say a flock of birds tilting mid-flight
and I say some performances we turn to long enough
to forget what we can never have, not without shedding
either or both of us. As if one had to clear out room

for a discovery that doesn't come so much as splinter
into the shag. We are down on our hands and knees
trawling gold acrylic pile. We are old here already.
To have rehearsed this almost infinitely hasn't helped
move things along. On the contrary. The whole idea

of perfection, evidently our aim, seems to have done
less to guide us away from missteps than to make them
even sharper, more palpable, and in several respects
downright impossible to avoid. (All the pressing in of
what we'll never have reminds us of how thoroughly

bereft we are, even of a hope of one day not wanting.)
You ought to put an end to this. (What pierces my hand
pierces yours, stops us into focus strong enough only
to drive off gauzy voices urging more harm for the quiet
that comes after.) You ought to have put an end to it

first. Shown a little courtesy. (Light dim as light can be
and still be thought light flosses the cleft between poorly
drawn curtains.) You shouldn't have followed me here.
You made it impossible not to. Took you long enough
to say it though. Some things go without. Without? Without

saying altogether. They sit unsaid in a lost auditorium,
muttering into night. I think they should be heard. I think
I can hear them now. As from behind a wall, or within it.
We have that gift. Yes, and each other. Also sticktoitiveness.
But it's gifts like these that always get one into trouble.

HIS
APOLOGIA

(handwritten: Latin:)

(handwritten note: I sentence — one complete thought)

As I press my ear against
earth or any surface

(handwritten: harsh break)

come to think of it I hear
the glissando of falling in
forgottenness then
worse—as, for example,

(handwritten: — em stopped line)

somewhere in Nebraska,
lodged in the throat
of an abandoned mineshaft
shut with a concrete
slab in the fall, warmed
by the gradual advance

(handwritten note: •Imagery → this sentence is captivating because it gives us a place and creates mystery with "abandoned mineshaft.")

of sun, a colony of dormant
bats awakens one
quiver at a time, steadily
congesting the air with
vibration, opening
the thin leather fold of the

(handwritten: very harsh and unnatural break)

wings Linnaeus knew bore

    much less resemblance to

a bird's than to the quick

    human hands held over a mouth

      red with attempt

    to cry out in danger or

those that have penned us

    in the din into which

we at once unhinge—and from

    which I can never tear

      myself away without

    what I agree to call irritability.

I think an author would have harsh, unnatural pauses to emphasize their thought process and to slow it down. Without breaks it wouldnt have the same meaning.

TO HIS DETRIMENT

Your wisdom is in never wearing me down entirely.
The way you leave me just enough to build upon, no more:
a pair of human hands to reach and push away with;

tightened chestfuls of remembrance; an alarum in my ear
which means I am awake now, means I am alive:
again despite appearances, again as though the day

had some contraption up its sleeve, another devilish design
time unfastens by degrees, almost teasingly in fact,
so that somewhere over lunch, as the whole becomes

discernible through the parts I'm given access to, I end up
wishing it upon myself: I wish it right up to the neck
but never any higher. Leave me will enough and strength,

I will never wish it higher! Frazzled aureate, the early
morning splits open like upholstery, a John-of-Patmos chintz.
I commend it all for happening, no matter what it is:

mint condition of a fountain, mindless under thunderclaps
and all these empty days, days crashing into phrases,
dawn conniption in the trees. The mere fact the fabric

of the air undoes itself intoxicates, that weariness before
having borne any burden, you leave me little choice:
I have to admire it; I drop my magazine. But as fertility

in domestic animals and plants was once held to decrease
in inverse ratio to food supply, I worry that my own
productivity might suffer in accordance with my appetite

for atmospheric disturbance, and I turn from the window
hungry for accomplishment, recalling the industry
exhibited once by a bone-pale spider, how it mended its web

in the rococo of an antique lectern, utterly immune
to the fluttering above it—a perfect miniature of tidiness!
Regarding miniatures, I notice several near at hand:

three of which I cherish, another which I recognize but lack
significant attachment to, a fifth which I renounce,
a sixth which you have placed here simply to disarm me,

and a seventh which belongs not to the category
of the miniature per se, but rather to that of the play of light on water.
My impulse to destroy all seven of the miniatures,

including those I cherish, including light on water,
I now understand as a passion for remembering
how delicate they are, and it need not find expression.

As I have come to understand it, tidiness is a form
of knowledge concerning the fine placement of things,
reminiscent of mosaics, or of the slow holy work

of rearranging a living space to find out what it means.
Hope is both product of and fuel for these machines,
and while you leave me little, you grant me near enough

to travel abroad in search of much more, a cache
perhaps mismanaged by those whose whole approach
undermines mine, and if I am not now that force

which only yesterday moved heavy furniture, my purpose
still precedes me: to journey forth by day, absorbing
hope from all passersby; to know the world's big backslap

unhampered by the steam of this or any downpour.
Farewell mirror where I tremble, farewell funny door
I bolt behind me—these are the unstoppable footsteps

whose return will herald such renaissance, I see no reason
to forestall it: a pivot, and I'm home again at last!
Dear detriment, see me through this victory. It is almost too rich.

There will be drink in this ceremony. We will prove such music.
What transport, markets, and livestock we have missed
we will enumerate, and somewhere in the adding, experience.

Time and again I have been this person we are gathered
here to celebrate, you'd think I would get used to it.
This pair of human hands to reach and push away with,

small wonder they are mine: I know just what to do with them.
Certain whitespace surrounds our sentences at first,
but with the whiskey things take off. In my dizziness to see

your wisdom clearly it grounds me. We need each other.
Without me you would cease to be yourself. Without you
I would be unthinkable. You ask me to comment on my triumph,

on rivers meandering across continents, on the imponderable
seas which receive these waters without remuneration,
but you make it sound so tedious! In the ultimate eloquent

gesture I reach out for small comforts, everyday items:
an unread book, urban water, any refreshment, but my touch
dissolves them. No other way to put it. I reach for them

and then they just aren't there. I try not to make too much of it.
Always it ends like this, in diminuendo, a heaving down.
I'd never do anything to hurt the miniatures, you know that.

I sense a change about to last, a shadow inching inward
toward the center of the pool, but then that old alarum
in my ear starts in again, a stillness fills the room. Evidently

my purpose is to maintain it. Now and then I shift somewhat
back and forth to throw the too-perfect stillness into relief.
But this is more than just maintenance. This is enhancement.

CHAPTER
FOR KINDLING
A TORCH

Who will fault me
    for not accepting
the responsibility
    of making meaning

from whatever it is
    you have somewhat
mysteriously laid
    before me when

the reason I picked it
    up for to begin with
was a hope of taking
    pleasure in the same.

EXPLANATION OF AN ORIOLE

Miraculous to find time to do nothing other than gather
dust like the mismatched furniture in whose slow company
my gratitude increases the longer I don't think about me:
no cringe at what I've done, no wince at what's to do.

Windowed oak grow bare in the time it takes to remember
the word for the small, sensitive branches that reach out
tirelessly from a nerve cell to receive adjacent nerve cells'
tidings of electricity and with dispatch pulse them back.

Another hour on standstill and I'll almost be able to feel
entangled in exchange with much more than necessary.
To notice wind incite the branches to interact in a manner
mistakable for happiness when happiness has stopped

seeming so implausible. Just to see the gold bolt through air
is explanation enough, a knowledge that opens itself up
without ending, an end in itself without having to conclude.
Just to breathe on purpose is an act of faith in this world.

BULLETIN FROM UNDER THE BED

Then it all starts seeming like a terrible mistake
    but to turn back now would only serve to make

matters even worse, bringing as it would the very
    seeming of the first condition into finitude, hastily

plastering it in history, and thereby giving shape
    where shapelessness has so long worked to our advantage.

It falls upon us then to build up our resistance to
    the lure of such reversal, letting what has seemed

plow ahead with its seeming without interruption,
    lest we find ourselves sent on the infinitely more

lamentable mission of having to confront what what
    began in mere seeming has managed to become, or—

while I hunt for the term for the left hand reaching out
    to prevent any further involvement of the curtain

ceremoniously you shield a last candle with your right
    against the wind released through the turning of pages.

DREAM OF
A POETRY
OF DEFENSE

As pendulum. As wind. As an ever-changing mutual voice.
As consciousness, sympathies, chords of speculation.
As to prolong speculation plastic and within. As copious

as infancy. As infrastructure to the most invisible
indestructible flower. And infinite. As infinite as pleasure
apprehended through excess. As cross-fertilization

of intelligence and cloud. And as light, and as energy.
As all related instruments indispensable to choruses.
As being differently indispensable. As being harmonious.

Whatever echo, cadence, or strain from the catalogue
of meaningful music, deep in the midst of its composition:
a proposal for living, an epitome, a permanent spark

through American darkness, barbarous as nightingale
awakened in a laboratory, hidden from the world
in its thousand details. As ancient armor around the body

deformed by protection. As pains against fragments
in an epoch of drama. As danger period, a distorted history.
As dance without music, as passion without capacity.

As exactness equal to any example. As under this thin
guise of circumstance. As if internal Minneapolis.
As enlarged by sorrow, terror, wheresoever I decline.

As against decay of liberties, as against misapplication,
monster propagating and the extinction of softness.
As overzealous as a number. As when the degradation

distributes itself as workforce venom, paralyzing
citizens in vivid architecture. As from the great faculty
an effluence is set forth. As episodes, as footsteps.

Whatever evil agencies will thicken and exacerbate.
Bewildered anomalies. Extraordinary drawbacks.
As convulsions nourishing their course with strength,

and expeditiously. As national vapors. As theater wrecks.
As at successive intervals the exhausted population
penetrated caverns. At drowse. At impossible to feel.

The full extent of sympathy considered a mistake.
As the dregs in the sensible. As in paradise stamped
in sleepless surveillance and proceedings of state.

But at inmost, a starry flock. At connection, an attaché.
And the still overflowing inextinguishable source.
As first written waters, as burning information.

We can advance the fountain. We can define foundation.
As awakened a shadow, as a vessel of assurance.
Let portions of our being. Let chapter the invention.

We want more brightness than money can imagine.
We want what arises from the passages between
mind management and the exasperation of anatomy.

Yoke evanescent wonder. Reanimate the blunted.
The mind that directs the hand is not vanishing.
Let laundering. Let mechanism turn to potable song

and highest human flight. As illustrious as trumpets
awakening washed garments. As manifestations
of the long electric work. Let gathering a nation.

Let the end of the battle be astonished birth of person.

4

THROUGH THE
WILDERNESS OF
HIS FOREHEAD

You wager too much, small self, on the way you feel. Nothing
  you have thought should last forever can't be lost.

Even the yellow wind that begins at once to strip the last of the
  heart-shaped foliage from the tree across the way

knows that feeling is a spell from which the mind can
  rouse itself awake if it would only let itself be taken

leaf by leaf apart. And you have felt this fear before, clung
  as to a vapor misremembering what had stood to

live through memory alone. Or was it afterwards among
  fog folded into blankets of some self-erasing sleep.

Or when, conversely, focused on the constancy of any given
  thing without dispersing, undissolved—an icecap-

white moon or clock-face on a tower—the mind intent on far
  too fine a point to take in any more. You will outlive

yourself again, and what you feel now, this adamantine
  sorrow, will scatter its dicethrow behind you into swans.

GLOBUS HYSTERICUS

1

A pity the selfsame vehicle that spirits me away from
factories of tedium should likewise serve to drag
me backwards into panic, or that panic should erect

massive factories of its own, their virulent pollutants
havocking loved waterways, frothing all the reed-
fringed margins acid pink and gathering in the shell

and soft tissues of the snails unknowingly in danger
as they inch up stems. Through the bulkhead door
I can hear their spirals plunk into the sluggish south-

bound current and dissolve therein with such brutal
regularity their dying has given rise to the custom
of measuring time here in a unit known as the snailsdeath.

The snailsdeath refers to the average length of time,
about 43 seconds, elapsing between the loss of the first
snail to toxic waters and the loss of the next, roughly

equivalent to the pause between swallows in a human
throat, while the adverb *here* refers to my person
and all its outskirts, beginning on the so-called cellular

level extending more or less undaunted all the way down
to the vale at the foot of the bed. I often fear I'll wake
to find you waiting there and won't know how to speak

on the subject of my production, or rather my woeful
lack thereof, but in your absence, once again, I will begin
drafting apologies in a language ineffectual as doves.

2

Daybreak on my marshland: a single egret, blotched,
trudges through the froth. I take its photograph
from the rooftop observation deck from which I watch

day's delivery trucks advance. I take advantage of
the quiet before their arrival to organize my thoughts
on the paranormal thusly: (1) If the human psyche

has proven spirited enough to produce such a range
of material effects upon what we'll call the closed
system of its custodial body, indeed if it's expected to,

and (2) If such effects might be thought to constitute
the physical expression of that psyche, an emanation
willed into matter in a manner not unlike a brand-

new car or cream-filled cake or disposable camera,
and (3) If the system of the body can be swapped out
for another, maybe an abandoned factory or a vale,

then might it not also prove possible for the psyche
by aptitude or lather or sheer circumstance to impress
its thumbprint on some other system, a production

in the basement, or in a video store, as when I find you
inching up steps or down a shady aisle or pathway,
dragging your long chains behind you most morosely

if you ask me, the question is: Did you choose this, or was it
imposed on you, but even as I ask your hands move
wildly about your throat to indicate you cannot speak.

3

After the memory of the trucks withdrawing heavy
with their cargo fans out and fades into late-morning
hunger, I relocate in time to the lit bank of vending

machines still humming in the staff-room corner for a light
meal of cheese curls, orange soda, and what history
will come to mourn as the last two cream-filled cakes.

Eating in silence, a breeze in the half-light, absently
thinking of trying not to think, I imagine the Bethlehem
steel smokestacks above me piping nonstop, the sky

wide open without any question, steam and dioxides
of carbon and sulfur, hands pressed to the wall as I walk
down the corridor to stop myself from falling awake

again on the floor in embarrassment. If there's any use
of imagination more productive or time less painful
it hasn't tried hard enough to push through to find me

wandering the wings of a ghost-run factory as Earth
approaches the dark vale cut in the heart of the galaxy.
Taking shots of the sunbaked fields of putrefaction

visible from the observation deck. Hoping to capture
what I can point to as the way it feels. Sensing my hand
in what I push away. Watching it dissolve into plumes

rising like aerosols, or like ghosts of indigenous peoples,
or the lump in the throat to keep me from saying that
surviving almost everything has felt like having killed it.

4

(*Plunk*) Up from the floor with the sun to the sound of
dawn's first sacrifice to the residues of commerce.
On autofog, on disbelief: rejuvenation in a boxer brief

crashed three miles wide in the waves off Madagascar,
cause of great flooding in the Bible and in *Gilgamesh*.
Massive sphere of rock and ice, of all events in history

(*Plunk*) thought to be the lethalmost. A snailsdeath
semiquavers from pang to ghost where the habit of ghosts
of inhabiting timepieces, of conniving their phantom

tendrils through parlor air and into the escapements
of some inoperative heirloom clock on a mantel shows
not the dead's ongoing interest in their old adversary

(*Plunk*) time so much as an urge to return to the hard
mechanical kind of being. An erotic longing to reanimate
the long-inert pendulum. As I have felt you banging

nights in my machine, jostling the salt from a pretzel.
This passion for the material realm after death however
refuses to be reconciled with a willingness to destroy

(*Plunk*) it while alive. When the last of the human voices
told me what I had to do, they rattled off a shopping
list of artifacts they wanted thrown down open throats.

That left me feeling in on it, chosen, a real fun-time guy
albeit somewhat sleep-deprived; detail-oriented, modern,
yes, but also dubious, maudlin, bedridden, speechless.

5

Graffiti on the stonework around the service entrance
makes the doorway at night look like the mystagogic
mouth of a big beast, amphibious, outfitted with fangs,

snout, the suggestion of a tongue, throat, and alimentary
canal leading to a complex of caves, tunnels, temples . . .
There are rooms I won't enter, at whose threshold I say

this is as far as I go, no farther, almost as if I can sense
there's something in there I don't want to see, or for which
to see means having wanted already to forget, unless

stepping into the mouth at last, pressed into its damp,
the advantage of not knowing is swapped out for the loss
of apartness from what you'd held unknown, meaning

you don't come to know it so much as become it, wholly
warping into its absorbent fold. I can't let that happen
if it hasn't already. What draws me on might be thought

canine, keen-sighted, but it's still incapable of divining why
the constant hum around or inside me has to choose
among being a nocturne of toxic manufacture, the call

of what remains of the jungle, or else just another prank
on my gullible anatomy. Am I not now beset in the utmost
basement of industry? Is that basement itself not beset

by the broad, black-green, waxy leaves of Mesoamerica?
And haven't I parted those selfsame leaves, discovering me
asleep on my own weapon, threat to no one but myself?

6

Asked again what I miss the most about my former life,
I remember to pause this time, look left, a little off-camera
an entire snailsdeath, an air of sifting the possibilities,

I eliminate certain objects and events from the running
right off the bat, such as when their great displeasure
brought the gods to turn to darkness all that had been

light, submerging mountaintops in stormwater, the gods
shocked by their own power, and heartsick to watch
their once dear people stippling the surf like little fishes.

Or when the flaming peccary of a comet struck the earth
with much the same effect, waves as high as ziggurats
crashing mathematically against our coastlines, scalding

plumes of vapor and aerosols tossed into the atmosphere
spawning storms to pummel the far side of the earth,
approximately 80 percent of all life vanished in a week.

Or when we squandered that very earth and shat on it
with much the same effect, and more or less on purpose,
emitting nonstop gases in the flow of our production,

shoveling it in as ancient icecaps melted, what difference
could another make now. And so I clear my throat, look
directly into the camera, and even though it will make me

come off bovine in their eyes, I say that what I miss the most
has to be those cream-filled cakes I used to like, but then
they prod me with their volts and lead me back to the barn.

7

After the panic grew more or less customary, the pity
dissolved into a mobile fogbank, dense, reducing visibility
from the rooftop observation deck. Mobile in the sense

that it possessed mobility, not in the sense that it actually
moved. Because it didn't. It just stayed there, reducing
visibility but not in the sense that it simply diminished it

or diminished it partly. Because it didn't. It pretty much
managed to do away with it altogether, as my photography
will come to show: field after field of untouched white.

After the possibility of change grew funny, threadbare,
too embarrassing to be with, I eased into the knowledge
that you'd never appear at the foot of the bed, the vale

turned into a lifetime's heap of laundry, and not the gentle
tuffets and streambanks of an afterlife it seems we only
imagined remembering, that watercolor done in greens

and about which I predicted its monotony of fair weather
over time might deaden one all over again, unless being
changed with death means not only changing past change

but past even the wish for it. I worried to aspire towards
that condition might actually dull one's aptitude for change.
That I would grow to protect what I wished to keep from

change at the cost of perpetuating much that required it.
In this sense I had come to resemble the fogbank, at once
given to motion but no less motionless than its photograph.

The last time I saw myself alive, I drew the curtain back
from the bed, stood by my sleeping body. I felt tenderness
towards it. I knew how long it had waited, and how little

time remained for it to prepare its bundle of grave-goods.
When I tried to speak, rather than my voice, my mouth
released the tight, distinctive shriek of an aerophone of clay.

I wanted to stop the shock of that from taking away from
what I felt. I couldn't quite manage it. Even at this late hour,
even here, the purity of a feeling is ruined by the world.

8

The noises from the basement were not auspicious noises.
I wanted to live forever. I wanted to live forever and die
right then and there. I had heard the tight, distinctive shriek.

Here again and now. I no longer have legs. I am sleeping.
Long tendrils of tobacco smoke, composed of carbon dioxide,
water vapor, ammonia, nitrogen oxide, hydrogen cyanide,

and 4,000 other chemical compounds, penetrate the room
through the gap beneath the door and through heating vents
with confidence. They are the spectral forms of anaconda.

The ruler of the underworld smokes cigars. A certain brand.
Hand-rolled. He smiles as if there is much to smile about.
And there is. He is hollow-eyed, toothless. His hat, infamous:

broad-brimmed, embellished with feathers, a live macaw.
His cape is depicted, often, as a length of fabric in distinctive
black and white chevrons. Otherwise, as here, the full pelt

of a jaguar. On a barge of plywood and empty milk cartons
he trudges through the froth. He is the lord of black sorcery
and lord of percussion. He is patron of commerce. He parts

the leaves of Mesoamerica, traveling with a retinue of drunken
ax wielders, collection agents. His scribe is a white rabbit.
Daughter of moon and of night. Elsewhere, you are having

your teeth taken out. There is no music left, but I still feel held captive by the cinema, and in its custom, I believe myself capable of protecting myself by hiding my face in my hands.

THE LAST
VIBRATIONS

Meanwhile we wanted the sentence to continue
fading as we thought another would begin
only after the first had finished and the last
vibrations seemed not to extend from the sentence
anymore but the fact that we had heard it
fading there together. The air off the river
remembered our being someplace else, or a time
behind us waiting to return, and the chill
presented its case for returning, knowing
what happened next must somehow depend
on dismantling much of what happened before.
Therefore we tried to prolong the sentence
to give ourselves time to decide by repeating it.
Time to decide. We knew that we couldn't
determine what happened down to the detail
but felt we might determine how the mind
should turn to meet it, the mind having often
believed itself to be struggling to continue
or thought itself that struggle to begin with.
In time to put that thinking aside, we thought
yellow leaves had torn through the blue
partitioned into day, but it was nowhere apparent
that they had. Down a channel of houses
framed in river air, we thought we could see

a portion of the water, but what we took for water
had foiled itself into a field of yellow light.
We knew that we might go on like that forever
without progression because the thought of
moving forward kept holding us back, the way
the thought of keeping still made us want to throw
ourselves like light on the river, unburdened
of that thinking we imagined might extend
endlessly thereafter, the way we thought we wanted it.
Light, river, air. Through the time we made
we felt what happened dismantle into yellow
leaves thought prolonged into trembling sentences.
Thought, leaves, houses; the last vibrations
faded to be remembered, in a place we would never
finish imagining: and it was then we began.

CHAPTER FOR REMOVING FOOLISH SPEECH FROM THE MOUTH

Tuning in again to the long elaborate
talk of the dead, ear held to a glass held
to what's left of the world, I let them
lullaby me back to where it all got under-
way: sick day centered on a little bed,

papered walls my sphere, birdsong's
infinite punctures in air like ticker tape
from the branches' fine interweaving.
I don't think to worry here whether half-
truths and music serve to reveal truth

or else only confuse it as stiff breezes
prove emphatic with their first purple
hyacinth and diesel. To what extent
stating a truth implies an endorsement
or when to embrace mere statement

means calling it true. I name the bees
sun's diplomats to an embassy of flowers
whether neighbors want me to or not.
Latest clouds in apricot coach my lips
through wordless chants against a purr

fuming from the nearby textile factory.
I'm not moving a muscle. Any exercise
to the tune of work will have to wait
for habit's stratocumulus to overcast this
puny light and need to stuff my mouth

with bargain cottons. When I'm done
I will be done, and the dead will come
riding their bone boomerang to return
me to that vertical life: tentative at first,
then all at once, as one might remove

red bandages at night, hands dutifully
maneuvering me forward as they take
me to task for having squandered so much
time on that sinkhole reverie I might
have invested in real estate or futures.

HIS
THEOGONY

In the bathtub I envision
    twin deities suppressing
the same eternal yawn.

Tiny handprints prance
    across their tightened lids.
Trembling beneath this

revelation, dozens more
    wait to hatch, but I lack
the wherewithal to make them.

As I sink back thinking
    they can all just imagine
themselves themselves

tonight, the twins' eyes pop
    open like the massive
tambourines of the future!

In this life I'll almost certainly
    not be acquainted with
much luxury, so if it ever

shakes in front of me again,
    I'll take it in my hands
posthaste: to play with, then destroy.

TIBERIUS
AT THE
VILLA JOVIS

Disturbances that ask to be likened to the weather
choose a storm that is wheeling nearer to oneself,
eye tightening through days across the tossed water
then upon one with its tentacles finagling the last
ramparts cracked open in a haze from cleft slumber.

Suppose a chance fear proved demon with devices
conducting one through mazes in unbroken sleep:
what happens one knows, but only with a knowing
mistakable for dream, or for a portraiture of weather
pushpinned to the wall above a bed's tangled deep.

Rescue from that knot must appear at first certain
danger leapt through a howl in full guise of storm,
then chipped at the ears by its own demonstration
as bedside necks with comfort's faces stuck on them
suffer love more acutely than if kept behind glass.

In that case to awaken would mean to tumble into
the storm you had run from: no stairway, no porthole
other than that which you find to climb out through
would mean to return to a need to be done, a mind
confined to its blizzard of quandary in time numbing

down, but not quite entirely—don't give up on me,
I can fight this, I am Tiberius, a sudden wooden boat
my boat floating sofa spoken from the mouth of a grotto
bright with water, the blue a blue noon sky, my voice
your voice is around us lacing with light's clear voices.

ADVICE TO BABOONS OF THE NEW KINGDOM

When they approach you with plates of soft fruit
and erotic objects, they have already singled you out

for worship. The agreeable arrangement of your face
and your humanlike behavioral traits have served

to identify you as a vessel for the habitation of gods.
Resist the impulse to play along, but if you can't,

and few can, enjoy the barge music as you drift up
the Nile from the Land of Punt—the many-stringed harps,

the delicate wooden flutes blown directly through
reinforced mouthpieces—all the while keeping close

watch on your ten attendants, who are glistening with
unguents made of rendered goat fat and spikenard.

As the barge nears the river's banks, leap from deck
into dense papyrus stalks that have attained a height

of no less than seven feet, certain that no crocodiles,
hippopotami, or comparable riparian predators lurk

half-submerged in shadows. If chance to abandon ship
fails to present itself, they will carry you into the city,

feed you pastilles of licorice and poppy, slowly bathe
and adorn you, anoint your thick, coarse, ash brown coat.

Afterwards, as the grogginess runs out, you return
to your senses in a dim-lit temple, your dietary needs

guessed at but missed, your body's dependence on
sunlight and freedom of movement unintuited as yet.

You grow despondent; your coat grows thin. You show
no evidence of divinity—does it need to be proven?

As you rest between ceremonies, watch the outlines
of your votaries interrupt the faint light at the mouth

of the corridor that leads from the temple's entrance down
to your holy chamber. In this manner, you will pass

months, whole seasons, possibly years, until you are
possessed of a god at last, and this one means business.

DREAM
OF THE
OVERLOOK

Already the present starts plotting its recurrence
    somewhere in the future, weaving what happens
in among our fabrics, launching its aroma, its music
    imbuing itself into floorboards, plaster, nothing can
stop it, it can't stop itself. You will never have access
    to its entirety, and you have asked how to calculate

what resists calculation, how to control what refuses
    to cooperate, but know full well a propensity to resist
and to refuse is the source of its power. The winters
    can be fantastically cruel, as if the weather can see
what happened here before and flares itself up as a way
    to remember, or else it intuits what evil is about

to happen and does what it can to divert it, stands on
    haunches to frighten it off. On the other hand maybe
what happens and the weather are working together,
    and one does what it can to push the other one up
over mountains, across a carpet. All this calculating
    exactness of modern life, one result of our monetary

economy, shares an ideal with the natural sciences—
        namely, to transform the world into a math problem.
The air feels so different, one can smell the privilege
        emanating from a battery of pine—one must build
a fortress of it, all the best people, one gold afternoon
        unraveling through sleep into another: some visitors

complain of nausea, vertigo, chills, feelings of dread,
        confusion, but it's so beautiful here . . . hard to believe
a snowstorm could be that close. I want to go outside,
        stretch out in the sun. Yet to our north, to our west,
it's snowing and cold, and it's moving as if conveyed
        down corridors into rooms whose many tribal motifs

have amplified over decades into labyrinths invisible
        to the naked eye but solid nonetheless, so that to walk
through a door means to face a number of possibilities
        greatly circumscribed by history: left, right, left, right
to the immaculate bathroom from which much steam
        shall gallop; right, right, left, left to the improbably

large bed where one lies sleeping; right, left, left, right
        to a window overlooking the hedge maze into which
somewhere in the future, quieter and away from what
        habits have kept us from feeling what static has kept us
going, unknowingly, we venture. Each of us a creature
        whose existence depends upon difference, our minds

discovering themselves in the differences between
present impressions and those that have preceded.
I think it might be a good idea if you leave the radio
on all the time now. The torrents keep building up
against a barrier far too fatigued to withstand much
more. As if at any minute. As if even the snow, falling,

possessed a little consciousness, near-infinite voices
boisterous with parenting advice, spiritual guidance,
stock tips, ribaldry, and grievances from the long lost.
No less as ghosts we consume ourselves in press.
Let me explain something to you. Many years from now,
on the verge of sleep, someone will be lying down

where I am lying now, and he or she will suffer, suddenly,
what I am suffering now, and where I come from,
we call that success. One must first become open, flung
wide or pried apart, to an order of feeling foreign
to most, a form of surrender to thought and occurrence
through apparatus not your own, hours of rendezvous

with the absent, the air, the demonic. Obviously some
people can be put off by the idea of staying alone
in a place where something like that actually happened
once, much less one where it happens all the time,
but when we reckon ourselves haunted, it is beyond
mere house. Now hold your eyes still so that I can see.

Midnight: the construction draws attention to its secret
　　passages; in intimate office, a wisdom is revealed
in the periphrasis a finance counselor laps from a lap.
　　The stars: and quiet, through evening's hush, a stranger
murmuring tranquillity to those closed in the narrow
　　cell arousing beyond or before more bourbon takes.

And you: that voice from afar, a flow of warm waves
　　I drift off remembering, that radiance through clouds
archaically measured in foot-candles: I think you hurt
　　my head real bad. Admittedly you're under binding
contract to do so. On the flipside much of the damage
　　has animated production of the interior as I know it,

made me more myself making brute with me, kindling
　　them old predatory embers never quite satisfactorily
displaced into numbers, as off in the distance, almost
　　picturesquely, the blizzard obliterates the humming
topography of Colorado, the hard writing of the place:
　　one sentence reconfigured page after page, no progress

but insistence, an entity meant in the plural, not single
　　wolves but a pack: in believing oneself to be just one
one made the first mistake. I think the next is to think
　　of the ax in our hands, blood everywhere, rather than
just pick it up, get on with it. One's economic interests
　　don't tell me to smother the beast in me, they tell us

to put it to work. I and the others have come to believe
somewhere in the future it will be just like nothing
ever happened, or like the sound of the horn at the heart
of nowhere. Notice the group photo in which I stand
apart from but attached to. I feel I should die if I let myself
be drawn into the center no less than if I just let go.

TEAM OF FAKE DEITIES ARRANGED ON AN ORANGE PLATE

[handwritten: → internal conflict]

[handwritten: → avoidance of activity → laziness]

Maybe indolence is a form of conflict between oneself

and everything else in the room, and turning

inward and away is a step toward peace, or into it. *[handwritten: — end-stopped]*

[handwritten: ↳ more sentences = slower read]   *[handwritten: ↳ tone of reflection and almost meditating. I would read more to see his overall message.]*

Or maybe peace would be more like turning

toward with hands outstretched, an open look

through measured breathing. Either way, I like it.

I know I do. I like the way it sounds when I sing.   *[handwritten: what is similar from His Apologia to this poem?]*

I like to see amber light from the pages

of the book I'm not reading. I like the clock's unstoppable *[handwritten: ↳ the line structure is significantly different & I feel like this has a softer and more appealing tone.]*

escapement and the cornstalks wrung with blue

convolvulus, a treacherous vine whose flowers

look like drunken trumpets. Look at that look on the face

[handwritten: Image 1: form of conflict]
[handwritten: Image 2: in the room]
[handwritten: Image 3: step forward]
[handwritten: ↳ what do these images do/create for you?]
[handwritten: These images make me think of confronting fearful things and maybe taking a step forwards discomfort?]

of the hardworking workman home again from work.
He's earned it. Look at that Indian elephant
decimating peppermints. I like it. I like what I see

and I am not indolent. I like a nonexistent Deity
and a team of fake deities arranged on an orange plate.
I like what I've done though I know it won't last.

And even if there is a Deity, I still like the idea
of a team of little fakes, and if we turn their invention
into a contest, you can bet your ass I'm winning.

CHAPTER FOR
A HEADREST

The flat base, the straight shaft, the neckpiece
    curved to accommodate the head, the wood

type indeterminate; often funerary, possibly
    an item of everyday use; as early as the First

Dynasty through the Ptolemaic period, little change
    in three millennia: let the barge push . . .

When the mind refuses to stop expanding
    arguments between itself and the particular

instance into a single, half-articulate drama
    about the self and all the wearing it must suffer;

when they call on me—and they will—
    through the workweek, on speakerphone

deep in the in-box or underground wandering
    beyond the far the balladeer called fond—

tell them this: that the infinitesimal portion of the blue
    planet's mass that answered to my name

wanted never to drag its ass out of bed again.
    Lost aptitude for the throng and being

thrown through the clear-air turbulence of it.
    Found hospice in some box of frozen music.

Found the deity who, intent on disappearing,
    assumed the form of an invisible giraffe

then hid itself beneath a pyramid of glass
    whose airtight walls fogged up in response

to the deity's breath, a development at once
    revealing *and* occluding our last known whereabouts.

(Or, to be brief, although brevity was never
    what we were after after all, tell them pigeons

have awakened my head at the horizon's chrome-
    spattered lapis—and it can't be reached.)

IN HIS TREE

They are untold: the advantages of entangling
oneself completely in a place like this, up and beyond
all chance of discovery, here where *untold* means
not *in the dark*, but *numberless*, *numberless* not
without number, but *many*—and if I sit in the dark
now and wait without number, the difference is

I do it voluntarily. Not the way the yellow leaf
is chased by another but the way the word *yellow*
can be drawn by hand through the same pond
air and then across an open page. Here the one keeps
evolving into the next, like listening into seeing
thin layer after layer of nacre affix to (to whelm)

the body fastened to sleep in the heart of a pearl.
All afternoon a feeling needed to be described to me
before I knew what I felt. The very terms of this
predicament had disqualified me from the honest
work of that description—prior to my knowledge of
how could I describe a thing?—while the whole

burden of assigning the work to a desk not my own
promised nothing but to deepen the predicament's
bite in my perception, and having watched hours
and even days turn out largely perceptual in the end
I would observe at this crossing no fast distinction
between seeming to be worse and actual worseness.

But an object absorptive of all my attention, a thing
outfitted with otherworldly fire, set to consume
more than I could ever feed it, might so completely
overtake the mind that there would be no room
available for feeling and therefore neither cause
nor way to describe what just wasn't there. And so

I set out to find that thing, drawn down by an under-
water instinct true to the warp and weft of a small
false deafness, locked deep in the blue-green private
compartment broken up into shifts and strung in
accordance to the wiles of arachnid light, a light too
truant from its source to reflect a compact back

with fidelity: the sun its half-remembered lozenge
trapped among the birch. Everywhere suddenly
rivalingly glinting like a new place to contemplate.
Cobbled paths linked by garden bridges arched
over the pond's narrows and ambled on to unusable
amphitheaters brightened by mats of continuous

aquatic vegetation: primarily macrophytic algae
fringed in eelgrass, coontail, and the American lotus
rising a child's height above the water's surface.
Suspended in the air on a firm stalk the enormous
round leaves shaped into bluish, soft-sided cups;
if floating, into plates; if emergent, they were as yet

unopened scrolls, a history of the pond's bottom
unnoticeably written on them. Portions of the lotus
interknit beneath the surface provided habitats
for invertebrates not visible from bridges: cryptic
rotifers and hydras, the larval and the nymph
incarnations of mosquitoes, beetles, damsel- and dragon-

flies fast as horses as adults, but in their youth
sustenance for numberless fish, amphibians, reptiles
and all the fervid waterfowl whose bills plunge
upward and down with untold destructiveness.
And I could tear my eyes from none of this, probably
because the mind kept seeing more than an eye

or kept wanting to, detecting in what it landed on
what it didn't see but knew, sensing the relation
between things present and between present things
and those remembered or supposed: humanity
in the park's stonework, messages raveled in
long bolts of music stampeding from the ancient

calliope at the heart of the carousel, and the future
bound in decay. A lost past beating in sago palm,
the hagiography of red caladium, and the resistance
to deterministic thoughts on identity implicit in
ten skipjacks convulsing from the shallows at once.
Always a stuntlike communiqué in the loop-the-

loop in which wind blows a paper cup across macadam,
deep in a mushroom, and in 108 sunflower faces
turned to face the setting sun, its diameter spanning
108 times that of the earth, here where we in turn
invest in 108 feelings: the first 36 pertaining to the past,
as many again to the present, and as many again

trailing off into the future, each coruscating dimly
as daystars, or as stars at night through exhaust, each
known by its own appellation, each with a unique
list of probable causes, cures, and a prolix description
reworked as history determines what we can feel.
All afternoon a feeling needed to be described to me

but the wording only veered it nearer to the word.
Or even just to check on it would change the way I felt.
Furthermore it constantly underwent self-started
evolutions I pretty much never managed to observe:
fluctuating on like a soft shifting mass, yielding
instantly to pressure and engulfing any object senseless

enough to have trusted in its surface, incorporating
whatever it can into the grand amalgam of itself
discovering itself and finding everything perfectly
indispensable and pointless as the rowboat comparison
builds for the landlocked hydrophobe in all of us.
Nothing terrestrial could be equal to a force like this.

No leathery general could ascertain its stratagem
squinting through binoculars across the scorched sands.
The TV might be getting warm, but police hounds
can't track it down because it smells like everything.
To surrender to it means you taste its invincibility
deliquescing in your dune-dry mouth, its properties

becoming yours, as when vigilant in a cherry tree
one converts into the branches, the drooping downy-
undersided leaves, the frail umbrella-like flowers
and impending fruit, until you forget what you were
watching for to begin with, the need to know now
culminating not in dominance, not control, but liberty.

CHAPTER
FOR NOT
DYING AGAIN

After will in the shape of an Egyptian plover pries me
loose from the teeth of a crocodile methodically
dozing in the netherworld's plug-in sun, I will come

back to you, World, wholehearted for the real, having
fed too long on its substitute. My lungs will plump
in actual air, my skin will pink, I'll be gone one minute

back in it in the next, and only half abashed as you
start ribbing me to death for thinking death could ever
be able to keep us from devouring each other when

even we can't stanch it. Archetypical picnic blanket
flattened in the dappling by the sun-flecked creek.
In an eyeblink, I'm all over it. You bring me: livestock

cut in portions, herbaceous intoxicants, a snowy mountain
peak made visible as the cloud cover thinks itself
over and dissipates. Tuna fish and breakfast flakes,

the lawn clippings' secret heat, bees in the foxglove,
celery, and 14.5 pounds per square inch of air pressure
here on land (a little more at sea). I bring you: room

and board for your infinite bacteria, parasites, and viruses.
Moreover, history has proven me your last available
amanuensis many nights, transcribing your vibrations

into jingles into morning. Times when I grow weary
of English sentences—the way they keep on insisting
something is something else, or something is doing

something to something else, or to itself, or nothing—
you let me hum. I'm humming now, counting the hours
until the plover carries me back in pieces in its beak.

Since my death, I'm not so anxious anymore. I can wait
like math on a damp day: my lone solution imminent
in the storm. But to have lived in you as I did, truly lovingly

despite big differences, should guarantee my passage
won't be long. Make it happen, and whatever you need,
I'll be there for you, you know that. Even if it kills me.

HIS FUTURE
AS ATTILA
THE HUN

But when I try to envision what it might be like to live
    detached from the circuitry that suffers me to crave

what I know I'll never need, or what I need but have
    in abundance already, I feel the cloud of food-court

breakfast loosen its embrace, I feel the shopping center
    drop as its escalator tenders me up to the story

intended for conference space. I feel my doubt diminish, my debt
    diminish; I feel a snow that falls on public statuary

doesn't do so sadly because it does so without profit.
    I feel less toxic. I feel the thought my only prospect

lies under a train for the coverage stop. Don't think I never
    thought that way because I have and do, all through

blank October a dollar in my pocket back and forth
    to university. Let the record not not show. I have

deserted me for what I lack and am not worth. All of this
    unfolds through episodes that pale as fast as others

gain from my inertia: I have watched, I'll keep watching
    out from under blankets as the days trip over the

days before out cold on the gold linoleum behind them
    where we make the others rich with sick persistence.

But when I try to envision what it might be like to change,
    I see three doors in front of me, and by implication

opportunity, rooms full of it as the mind itself is full
    thinking of a time before time was, or of the infinite

couch from which none part, and while the first two doors
    have their appeal, it's the third I like best, the one

behind which opens a meadow, vast, and in it, grazing
    on buttercups, an errant heifer with a wounded foot,

its bloody hoofprints followed by a curious shepherd back
    to something sharp in the grass, the point of a long

sword which, unearthed, the shepherd now polishes with
    his rodent-skin tunic, letting the Eurasian sun play

upon it for effect, a gift for me, a task, an instrument to lay
    waste to the empire now placed before me at my feet.

THE MALADY THAT TOOK THE PLACE OF THINKING refers to a photograph taken during the My Lai Massacre (1968).

THE NEW HYMNS is for Dawn Marie Knopf.

BETWEEN THE RIVERS is indebted to Philip Steele's *Eyewitness Mesopotamia* (2007).

CLAIR DE LUNE adapts Queen's Counsel member Philippe Sands's 2006 misquote of a statement made in 1946 via telegram by US diplomat George Kennan: "The greatest threat that can befall us as a nation is to become like those who seek to destroy us."

FUN FOR THE SHUT-IN takes its title from the last chapter of *Make and Do*, vol. eleven of *Childcraft: The How and Why Library* (1972).

THE CLOUD CORPORATION's fifth section reworks several passages from H. L. Mencken's "The Cult of Hope" (1920).

CHAPTER FOR BEING TRANSFORMED INTO A SPARROW, like the other "Chapter" poems in this book, takes its title from the Egyptian Book of the Dead.

THE LAST DREAM OF LIGHT RELEASED FROM SEAPORTS is composed of words selected from successive pages of the USA PATRIOT Act (2001) and from Bruce Springsteen's "Born to Run" (1975).

NO DIARY's italicized phrases are taken from chapter 8 of Charles Maturin's *Melmoth the Wanderer* (1820). The poem also borrows from the concluding paragraphs of Arthur Schopenhauer's 1851 essay "On the Vanity of Existence" (R. J. Hollingdale, trans.).

POEM BEGINNING WITH A SENTENCE FROM *THE MONK*'s title refers to the 1796 novel by Matthew Lewis.

THE RUMORED EXISTENCE OF OTHER PEOPLE is for Brett Fletcher Lauer.

THE NEW HISTRIONICISM adapts a medieval Irish anecdote as translated by Kenneth Hurlstone Jackson in his *A Celtic Miscellany* (1971). It also adapts a passage from the Rule of Saint Benedict (c. 530).

DREAM OF ARABIAN HILLBILLIES is composed of words selected from successive pages of Osama bin Laden's "Declaration of War Against the Americans Occupying the Land of the Two Holy Places" (1996) and randomly from the theme song to *The Beverly Hillbillies*, Paul Henning's "The Ballad of Jed Clampett" (1962).

TO HIS DETRIMENT adapts a few passages from Andrew Brown's translation of Gustave Flaubert's *Memoirs of a Madman* (1838).

DREAM OF A POETRY OF DEFENSE is composed of words selected from successive pages of Percy Bysshe Shelley's *A Defence of Poetry* (1821) and randomly from *The 9/11 Commission Report*, sec. 13.5, "Organizing America's Defenses in the United States" (2004).

DREAM OF THE OVERLOOK cites a few passages from Stanley Kubrick and Diane Johnson's screenplay of the movie *The Shining* (1980) and adapts a few from Edward Schils's translation of Georg Simmel's "The Metropolis and Mental Life" (1903).

HIS FUTURE AS ATTILA THE HUN's last sentence alludes to a fabled event in the life of Attila as related by Edward Gibbon in *The History of the Decline and Fall of the Roman Empire* (1776).

Many thanks to Mary Jo Bang, Lucie Brock-Broido, Robert Casper, Richard Howard, Geoffrey G. O'Brien, and especially Brett Fletcher Lauer and Lynn Melnick for their invaluable input and support throughout the writing of this book. Tremendous gratitude and thanks also to Matthew Zapruder.

Grateful acknowledgment is also made to the editors of the magazines in which versions of these poems first appeared: *American Poet*: To His Debt; *The Awl*: Antepenultimate Conflict with Self; His Future as Attila the Hun; *Boulevard*: Advice to Baboons of the New Kingdom; Through the Wilderness of His Forehead; *The Canary*: To His Detriment; *Coal Hill Review*: Dispatch from Behind the Mountain; *Columbia: A Journal of Literature and Art*: Chivas Regal; His Agenda; The New Hymns; The Night Ship; To His Own Device; *Columbia Poetry Review*: Fun for the Shut-in; *Crowd*: The New Intelligence; *Critical Quarterly*: No Diary; *Denver Quarterly*: Chapter for Being Transformed into a Lotus; Chapter for Breathing Air Among the Waters; Chapter for a Headrest; *Fence*: His Excuse; *Grist: The Journal for Writers*: Explanation of an Oriole; Montezuma to His Magicians; *Gulf Coast*: Fantasies of Management; His Theogony; No Mission Statement, No Strategic Plan; *Harper's*: The Cloud Corporation; *The Iowa Review*: Dream of the Overlook; The Rumored Existence of Other People; *Jerry*: Dream of Arabian Hillbillies; *jubilat*: The Last Dream of Light Released from Seaports; The Malady That Took the Place of Thinking; Team of Fake Deities Arranged on an Orange Plate; *Lana Turner*: Chapter for Not Dying Again; In His Tree; *The Literary Review*: Chapter for Being Transformed into a Sparrow; *Maggy*: Poem Beginning with a Sentence from *The Monk*; *Memorious*: Partial Inventory of Airborne Debris; *The Modern Review*: Dream of a

Poetry of Defense; *The Nation*: Clair de Lune; *The New Republic*: Chapter for Removing Foolish Speech from the Mouth; *The New York Review of Magazines*: Chapter for Kindling a Torch; *The Paris Review*: Globus Hystericus; *A Public Space*: Bled; The Last Vibrations.

Many thanks to Christian Lux, Barbara Thimm, and John Dilg, the publisher, translator, and illustrator, respectively, of *Die neue Sicht der Dinge: Gedicthe* (Luxbooks, 2008), in which some of these poems first appeared. Thanks also to Hand Held Editions for printing the book's title poem as a chapbook. Thanks, too, to Kristin Norderval and Ensemble π for setting "Clair de Lune" to music.

Thanks also to Michael Dumanis and Cate Marvin for including "The New Intelligence" in *Legitimate Dangers: American Poets of the New Century* (Sarabande, 2006), to Robert Strong for including "Chapter for Being Transformed into a Sparrow" in *Joyful Noise: An Anthology of American Spiritual Poetry* (Autumn House, 2006), and to Mark Irwin for including "Clair de Lune" and "Team of Fake Deities Arranged on an Orange Plate" in *13 Contemporary Younger American Poets* (Proem Press, 2010). Lastly, thanks to Don Selby and Diane Boller for featuring "Dream of a Poetry of Defense," "Globus Hystericus" and "The New Intelligence" on the *Poetry Daily* website.

TIMOTHY DONNELLY's first book of poems, *Twenty-seven Props for a Production of Eine Lebenszeit*, was published by Grove Press in 2003. He is a poetry editor for *Boston Review* and teaches at Columbia University's School of the Arts.